A NEW OWNER'S
GUIDE TO
SHETLAND
SHEEPDOGS

JG-144

Overleaf: A Shetland Sheepdog adult and puppy photographed by Isabelle Francais.

Opposite page: A Shetland Sheepdog owned by Bonnie Smith.

The publisher wishes to acknowledge the following owners of the dogs in this book: Daphne Allen, Karen Aurelius, Judy Brown, Candray Kennels, Joanne Chaplek, Rick and Linda Churchill, Cinder Glo Shelties, Robin Clemas, Tracey Denier, Peggy Duezabou, Kathy Dziegiel, Golden Hylite Shelties, Denise Gustafson, Rose Hartley, Judy Lang, Sherry Lee, Joyce Marciano, Joan McBurney, Trevor Parkin, William Polliey, Tina Ripley, Marguerite Salls, September Shelties, Ron and Bonnie Smith, Shirley Vicchitto, and Marilyn Weimer.

Photographers: Daphne Allen, Paulette Braun, Robin Clemas, Tara Darling, Isabelle Francais, Denise Gustafson, Jack Jurcak, Barbara Linden, S. Shane McConnell, Jan Peterson, Bonnie Smith, Judith E. Strom, Karen Taylor.

The author acknowledges the contribution of Judy Iby to the following chapters: Health Care, Sport of Purebred Dogs, Identification and Finding the Lost Dog, Traveling with Your Dog, and Behavior and Canine Communication.

© by T.F.H. Publications, Inc.

Distributed in the UNITED STATES to the Pet Trade by T.F.H. Publications, Inc., One T.F.H. Plaza, Neptune City, NJ 07753; on the Internet at www.tfh.com; in CANADA Rolf C. Hagen Inc., 3225 Sartelon St. Laurent-Montreal Quebec H4R 1E8; Pet Trade by H & L Pet Supplies Inc., 27 Kingston Crescent, Kitchener, Ontario N2B 2T6; in ENGLAND by T.F.H. Publications, PO Box 15, Waterlooville PO7 6BQ; in AUSTRALIA AND THE SOUTH PACIFIC by T.F.H. (Australia), Pty. Ltd., Box 149, Brookvale 2100 N.S.W., Australia; in NEW ZEALAND by Brooklands Aquarium Ltd. 5 McGiven Drive, New Plymouth, RD1 New Zealand; in SOUTH AFRICA, Rolf C. Hagen S.A. (PTY.) LTD. P.O. Box 201199, Durban North 4016, South Africa; in Japan by T.F.H. Publications, Japan—Jiro Tsuda, 10-12-3 Ohjidai, Sakura, Chiba 285, Japan. Published by T.F.H. Publications, Inc.

MANUFACTURED IN THE
UNITED STATES OF AMERICA
BY T.F.H. PUBLICATIONS, INC.

A NEW OWNER'S GUIDE TO
SHETLAND SHEEPDOGS

LINDA CHURCHILL

Contents

The Shetland Sheepdog's role in ranching and farming is legendary.

There is no end to what a well-trained Shetland Sheepdog can accomplish.

The Shetland Sheepdog is a wonderful addition to any family.

A Sheltie puppy is a lot of love in a small package.

The accomodating Sheltie can accompany you wherever you go.

HISTORY and Origin of the Shetland Sheepdog

Many people refer to the Shetland Sheepdog, or as it is commonly known—the Sheltie, as a miniature Collie or sometimes even as a toy Collie. This could not be further from the truth. Although there is indeed Collie blood coursing through the distant background of today's Shetland Sheepdog, the breed has bred true for many generations. The look of the two breeds is indeed similar, and their ancient histories are much the same, but the Sheltie's development takes an abrupt departure to the Shetland Islands which lie some 50 miles off the northernmost coast of Scotland. How the little dogs developed on the Shetland Islands helps one better understand the abilities and character of the breed.

The Shetland Sheepdog developed in the rugged Shetland Islands where he was valued as a hardy guardian and herder of livestock.

All dogs, regardless of breed, trace their origin to a common ancestor. Whether the breed is one of the purely decorative and diminutive toy breeds or a member of the stalwart working breeds, a dog's ancestry eventually takes it back to none other than *Canis lupis*—the wolf. The wolf's transition from creature of the forest to mankind's great friend and companion was born from mutual benefit.

In the dawn of civilization, just providing food for self and family and staying out of harm's way was undoubtedly the human population's major concern in life. This in itself was no mean feat, considering that use of even the most rudimentary tools was extremely limited at this stage of human development. There is little doubt that many of the wolf's social habits might have seemed strikingly familiar to the early humans and observation of the wolf's hunting habits could easily have taught man some effective hunting techniques to use himself. Wolves, on the other hand could have seen a

7

source of easily secured food in man's discards. The association grew from there.

THE WOLVES EVOLVE

As the relationship developed through the ages, certain descendants of these increasingly domesticated wolves could be advantageously selected to assist in hunting and other survival pursuits. The wolves that performed any function that lightened early human existence were cherished and allowed to breed, while those that were not helpful or whose temperament proved incompatible were driven away.

These wolves-cum-dogs were not only capable of deciding which game was most apt to be easy prey, they knew how to separate the chosen animal from the herd, and how to bring it to ground. These abilities did not escape the notice of man.

Few Shelties ever forget their original purpose. Pinetopnotch Silver Corvette, NA tends to his flock.

Richard and Alice Feinnes, authors of *The Natural History of Dogs*, classify most dogs as having descended from one of four major groups: the Dingo group, the Greyhound group, the Mastiff group and the Northern or Arctic group. Each of these groups trace back to separate and distinct branches of the wolf family.

The Arctic or Nordic group classification is made up of dogs that are direct descendants of the rugged northern wolf (*Canis lupis*). Included in the many breeds of this group are: the Arctic-type dogs such as the Alaskan Malamute and the Chow Chow, the Terriers, the Spitz-type dogs including Schipperkes and Corgis and the herding breeds. The gene pool of the Shetland Sheepdog includes both Spitz and herding-type descendants.

Almost all of the Northern group, like their undomesticated ancestors, maintained the characteristics that protect them from the harsh environment of the upper European countries. Weather-resistant coats were of the ideal texture to protect

After hundreds of years of working outdoors, the Sheltie is a robust resilient dog that adapts to all kinds of weather. Megan Strom and Blue Skye Splendor romp in the snow.

from rain and cold. There was a long coarse outercoat that shed snow and rain and a dense undercoat that insulated against sub-zero temperatures. These coats were especially abundant around the neck and chest thereby offering double protection for the vital organs.

Well-coated tails could cover and protect the nose and mouth should the animal be forced to sleep in the snow. Small ears were not as easily frostbitten or frozen as the large and pendulous ears of some of the other breeds. The muzzle had sufficient length to warm the frigid air before it reached the lungs. Leg length was sufficient to keep the chest and abdomen above the snow line. Tails were carried horizontally or up over the back rather than trailing behind in the snow.

This is not to indicate that there were no cross-breedings of the types nor that abilities peculiar to one group may not have also been possessed by another. In fact, it is believed that crosses to the Dingo descendants are what provided some of the Northern breeds with a more refined attitude and tractability.

With the passing of time humans realized they could manipulate breedings of these evolving wolves so that the resulting offspring became even more proficient in particular areas. While human populations developed a more sophisticated lifestyle, they also thought up new ways in which the domesticated wolves could be of assistance. Customizing the evolving wolves to suit growing human needs was the next step. They became hunting wolves, guard wolves, and herding wolves. The list of useful duties grew and grew.

ROMANS CLASSIFY THE BREEDS

One can find documentation of controlled breeding practices by Roman writers as early as the first century A.D. The Romans had

Am. Can. Ch. Tara Hill The Brass Chain owned by Ron and Bonnie Smith shows off his magnificent coat.

There is no end to the accomplishments and awards that can be achieved by the dedicated owner and the Sheltie.

actually broken down the various types of what could, by then, be referred to as *Canis familiaris*, the dog, into six general classifications. These groupings are very similar to the "variety groups" used as a classification method by the American Kennel Club today. Two thousand years ago Roman writers talked of "house guardian dogs, shepherd dogs, sporting dogs, war dogs, scent dogs, and sight dogs."

Descriptions of the shepherd and herding dogs that had descended from the Northern wolf can be found in Roman writings as early as 36 B.C. Many of their characteristics are distinctly similar to those of the modern working shepherd breeds. Granted, the dogs described were larger and fiercer than what is expected of the modern herding breeds, but in those early days the flock dogs were as much guardians as they were herders.

The Roman invasion of Britain introduced these flock guardians to the isles, where they continued to protect the stock of the settlers as they had on the Continent. The next wave of invaders to enter the British Isles emanated from Scandinavia. With them came another branch of the northern wolf descendants—the Spitz-type dogs. These dogs were typified by their Nordic characteristics—smaller in size than the Roman descendants and distinguished by their black-with-white or sable-with-white markings. The difference in size provided a more agile dog, and the white markings on the dogs' moving parts were particularly useful in a land where daylight hours were short and night work was not uncommon.

These workers of the flocks had no specific name, or at least none found its way into print, until 1617 when first mention of these "Collie dogs" is found in describing the habits of a Scottish bishop. The latter it seems was inclined to arrive for a visit at meal times like "a Collie dog." The actual Collie name has several explanations: the word "coalley" meaning black; the Welsh "coelius" meaning faithful or perhaps the Scottish variety of sheep known as the "colley."

"Horses For Courses"

In order to understand the diversity of the British herding dogs in general, mention should be made here of a formula used by British stockmen dating back into antiquity. These gifted men developed prize livestock guided by an old adage which stated simply, "horses for courses." That is, one should choose a formula that will produce a horse best suited to the terrain on which the horse will work. This formula was applied to breeding of all animals including dogs, and from it came some of the world's most outstanding dogs.

This breeding concept applied as much, if not more, to the rugged Shetland Islands that were populated by a small dark race of people called Picts. The Picts living there had need of a small, active, and industrious kind of dog to work the small island sheep. The inhospitable terrain and sparse vegetation of the Shetland Islands made economy of size of paramount concern with any living thing hoping to survive there. The island inhabitants were tenant farmers called crofters. Their homes were small crofts, sometimes called "toons," and for this reason their dogs, and the Shetland Sheepdogs of today, are often referred to as "Toonie" dogs.

At any rate, the dogs were primarily of Spitz descent. They were called Yakki dogs. Time, and need for working ability, was eventually to bring crosses to some of Britiain's small Collie breeds, and history even records the blood of a black and tan King Charles Spaniel was used to "improve" the breed. The need for "improvement" was no doubt stimulated at least in part by the fact that ladies from Queen Victoria's royal court had stopped on the islands and had taken a fancy to the prettier of the little dogs they saw there. The ladies brought some of the little dogs home with them and they became lap dogs. It is not unreasonable to assume the crofters tried to enhance the attractiveness of their dogs for commercial purpose. It was undoubtedly also at this time that crosses to the Pomeranian are known to have been made.

Regardless of attractiveness, or lack of it, the dogs that eventually evolved were rugged and hard working, blessed with an almost uncanny ability to make decisions regarding the welfare of the small sheep and ponies in their charge. Size and type were

Ride 'em cowboy! The Sheltie's contribution to ranching and farming is legendary.

The Shetland Sheepdog is an athletic dog who thrives on exercise and activity.

irregular as a result of the crosses to the many breeds of contradictory blood in their background. This inconsistency was exacerbated by yet another Collie cross at a later date, said to have been made in response to the importation of some larger variety sheep. These irregularities continue to plague the Shetland Sheepdog breed to this day.

The Spitz type dogs in the Sheltie's background can undoubtedly accept the blame for the pricked ears and tails inclined over the back. The King Charles Spaniel ears and coat did not help to standardize the little dog from the Shetland Isles either, but all in all, faults aside, they left the breed with one of the sweetest and most amiable dispositions that exist among purebred dogs. The faults contributed will no doubt be eradicated by dedicated breeders over the years but the breed's exquisite temperament will be cherished for all time to come.

The Breed Becomes Established

By the turn of the current century classes were provided for the little "Shetland Collies" at agricultural shows and organization of a club was under way. The stud book was officially set up in 1908 and the members of the Shetland Island Club decided that their breed should no longer be referred to as the Shetland Collie but rather as the Shetland Sheepdog, thus giving it permanent distinction from its herding Collie relatives.

Whether sheep, goat, or human, all charges are well protected under the watchful eye of the Shetland Sheepdog.

The Shetland Sheepdog Club placed itself under the authority of the Kennel Club in London making any changes to the club or to the breed invalid until approved by that organization. In 1914, The Kennel Club granted official recognition to the breed. Conflicting breed histories alternately credit the breed's first champions as Ch. Woodvold owned by Miss Beryl Thynne or Ch. Clifford Pat owned by Misses Dawson and Wilkinson.

The Shetland Sheepdog In America

Although Shetland Sheepdogs, or "Shetland Collies" as they were known then, may well have accompanied Scottish immigrants to America before 1910, it was not until that year that we have an official record of the breed's arrival and entry in the AKC stud book. At that time John G. Sherman, Jr. of New Rochelle, New York imported the male Lord Scott and the female Lerwick Bess.

In 1912, the first Shetland Sheepdogs were shown at the Westminster Kennel Club Dog Show. The sexes were combined at that show and Lerwick Bess was placed first. The next show for the breed was held at Nassau Kennel Club where the sexes were divided. Here another of J.G. Sherman's imports, Lerwick Rex, was selected Best of Breed. Rex went on to become the breed's first champion in America.

World War I curtailed breeding and showing in America and it was not until the early 1920s that Sheltie activities resumed in earnest. In September of 1921, Edward R. Stettinius imported Kilravock Lassie from England. Lassie was held in high regard by all who saw her and was in turn purchased by Catherine E. Coleman (later Catherine Coleman Moore) of Williamsburg, Massachusetts. Miss Coleman established her Sheltieland Kennels at that time and the kennel became one of the cornerstones of the breed in America. To her goes the credit for breeding Ch. Miss Blackie, the first American-bred champion.

A Sheltie's greatest love is for his family. Michelle Hanson with her best friend, Ch. Christy of Honeywood.

The Sheltie caught on in America with amazing rapidity. By 1929 the American Shetland Sheepdog Association (ASSA) held its first meeting, and applied for, and was granted recognition by the AKC just a few months later.

The ASSA held its first specialty show in conjunction with the famed Morris & Essex Kennel Club show in May of 1933. Edward McQuown judged an entry of 33 and selected Ch. Piccolo O'Pages Hill, owned by W. Gallagher, as Best of Breed.

With the exception of the years of World War II, during which all dog show activities were curtailed, interest and activity among Sheltie fanciers has steadily increased. In 1996, the breed ranked number 14 among the 143 breeds registered by the AKC. The breed has proven itself highly competitive in the conformation and obedience rings nationwide, as well as extremely proficient in herding trials and agility competition.

The little worker from the Shetland Islands has been fully embraced by dog fanciers of the world and has returned that acceptance with unquestionable devotion to every family in which the breed is owned.

Sheltie breeders have strived to preserve the breed's herding instincts and good temperament.

CHARACTERISTICS of the Shetland Sheepdog

I f you haven't fully decided whether or not to add a Sheltie puppy to your life, a visit to the home or kennel where there is a litter of puppies is probably not the best idea in the world—you will not leave without one! Sheltie puppies are absolutely irresistible. There is probably nothing quite so captivating as these little bundles of fluff.

For this very reason the person anticipating owning a Sheltie should give serious thought to the final decision. All puppies are cuddly and cute—Sheltie puppies particularly so with their angelic expressions. There is nothing more seductive than a litter of Shetland Sheepdog puppies at play or nestled together sound asleep, one on top of the other. But in addition to being cute, Sheltie puppies are living, breathing and very mischievous little creatures. Not only that, they are totally dependent upon their human owner for all their needs once they leave their mother and littermates.

Buying a dog, especially a puppy, before someone is absolutely sure they want to make that commitment can be a serious mistake. The prospective dog owner must clearly understand the amount of time and work involved in dog ownership. Failure to understand the extent of commitment dog ownership involves is one of the primary reasons there are

Sheltie puppies are hard to resist, so be sure your decision to own one is carefully considered. This Sheltie trio is owned by Judy Lang.

so many unwanted canines that are forced to end their lives in an animal shelter.

Before anyone contemplates the purchase of any dog there are some very basic conditions that must be considered. One of the first important questions that must be answered is whether or not the person who will ultimately be responsible for the dog's care and well being actually wants a dog.

The whole family must be committed to caring for your new Sheltie pup.

All too often it is the mother of the household who must shoulder the responsibility of the family dog's day-to-day care. While the children in the

The Sheltie is happiest in the company of people. Keri Smith cuddles with a bi-blue colored Sheltie pup named Blueberry Buttons.

family, perhaps even the father, may be wildly enthusiastic about having a dog, it must be remembered that they are away most of the day at school or work. It is often "mom" who will be taking on the additional responsibility of primary caregiver for the family dog. Somehow this seems to be the case even when there is a working mom in the family. In addition to her work away from home, there are all those household chores it appears only a mom can handle. Does she, in fact, share the enthusiasm for what could easily become another responsibility on her unending list?

Pets are a wonderful method of teaching children responsibility, but it should be remembered that the enthusiasm that inspires children to promise anything in order to have a new puppy may quickly wane. Who will take care of the puppy once the novelty wears off? Does that person want a dog?

In terms of grooming, the Sheltie is a high-maintenance dog. The time you want to spend on grooming should be a consideration before selecting a breed.

Desire to own a dog aside, does the lifestyle of the family actually provide for responsible dog ownership? If the entire family is away from home from early morning to late at night, who will provide for all of a puppy's needs? Feeding, exercise, outdoor access and the like can not be provided if no one is home.

Another important factor to consider is whether or not the breed of dog is suitable for the person or the family with which it will be living. A fully grown Sheltie can handle the rough and tumble play of young children. A very young Sheltie puppy may have difficulty in doing so.

The Shetland Sheepdog puppy is a miniature version of the adult.

Then too, there is the matter of hair. A luxuriously coated dog is certainly beautiful to behold, but all that hair takes a great deal of care. Brushing an adult Shetland Sheepdog requires time and patience.

As great as claims are for a Sheltie's intelligence and trainability, remember the new dog must be taught every household rule that it is to observe. Some dogs catch on more quickly than others, and puppies are just as inclined to forget or disregard lessons as young human children are.

CASE FOR THE PUREBRED DOG

As previously mentioned all puppies are cute. Not all puppies grow up to be particularly attractive adults. What is considered beauty by one person is not necessarily seen as attractive by another. It is almost impossible to determine what a mixed breed puppy will look like as an adult. Nor will it be possible to determine if the mixed breed puppy's temperament is suitable for the person, or family, who wishes to own it. If the puppy grows up to be too big, too hairy, or too active for the owner what then will happen to it?

Size and temperament can vary to a degree even within purebred dogs. Still, selective breeding over many generations has produced dogs giving the would-be-owner reasonable assurance of what the purebred puppy will look and act like as an adult. Esthetics completely aside, this predictability is more important than one might think.

Purebred puppies will grow up to look like their adult relatives and by and large they will behave pretty much like the rest of their family too. Any dog, mixed breed or not, has the potential to be a loving companion. However, the predictability of a purebred dog offers reasonable insurance that it will not only suit the owner's lifestyle but the person's esthetic demands as well.

Before you bring a Shetland Sheepdog puppy into your household, visit breeders and spend as much time with both puppies and adults as you can. Be sure that the adult Sheltie is the dog that appeals to you esthetically and temperamentally.

There is nothing more important to the Sheltie than the return of her loved ones. Cinder Glo Kimberly patiently awaits the arrival of her master.

CHARACTER

The Shetland Sheepdog has several personality traits that can be difficult to cope with if the owner is not careful to control them when the dog is still young. This is not to say that an older dog cannot be retrained, but it is a far less difficult job to avoid the problem ever occurring in puppyhood than it is to convince the adult Sheltie it no longer wants to behave in that way.

Some Shelties are not beyond having a stubborn streak. Those that do will test their owners over and over just to "make sure" you are adamant about their not doing something. What may be terribly cute behavior for a puppy may not be quite so much fun when that puppy reaches adulthood. The Sheltie remembers what it is taught, what it has gotten away with in the past, and how to go about doing it again.

With their high degree of intelligence, Shetland Sheepdogs tend to get bored easily. As a rule they are not a breed that can be left on their own continuously or kept outdoors alone. They are "people dogs" and denied the opportunity to be with those they love, Shelties can demand attention by becoming barkers. One of the Sheltie's finest qualities

One of the Sheltie's finest qualities is his desire to please his owners. Obviously, this little girl will do anything to keep her mistress happy.

is his desire to bond with and please his master. Not being allowed to do so can make even the best bred Sheltie unhappy and hard to live with.

A perfect example of the close bond that can exist between a Sheltie and his owner was my female whose name was Cassie. Cassie was my best friend and knew my every thought. She was completely tuned in to my every emotion. When I was sad or depressed and had been crying, she would sit really close by and attempt to lick away the tears from my face.

If I were to become angry with my husband or children, Cassie was first to beat a hasty retreat until my anger had subsided. Other than that she lived to be with me every moment of her life, whether that meant watching television, cooking, or watching me work at my desk.

This need to be close is very strong in the Shetland Sheepdog. In fact, they can be underfoot just when you have forgotten they are there. Dangerous for someone who is not agile! But this need is born out of love and there is never any doubt that your Sheltie loves you. The love a Sheltie has for his owner is absolutely unconditional. Even if that owner is unfair or inconsiderate, the Sheltie continues to love with unflagging intensity.

TRAINABILITY

It has often been said that separating character from working ability in the Shetland Sheepdog is an extremely difficult thing to do. In truth, it is nearly impossible. So many things the Sheltie is and does are quite simply inherited traits from the gene pool that gave us that hard-working, courageous, and highly intelligent stock dog of old.

Today's Sheltie that keeps track of the children in a family and guides them away from danger is not unlike what a good Sheltie of old was. The breed's need to be with his owner is most certainly a holdover from the time when there

Shelties are ideal guardians and natural "baby-sitters." They make wonderful playmates and companions for any child.

24

There are no limits to what a patient, consistent Shetland Sheepdog owner can accomplish with her dog.

would have been little purpose to a dog that would abandon his flock or the shepherd who shared the responsibility for the flock with the dog. The ease with which the Sheltie can be trained to heel, sometimes with no coaching at all, is simply a holdover from his herding days. Indeed, as Catherine Coleman Moore said in her classic work on the breed, *The Complete Shetland Sheepdog*, "...breed character is the direct development of the Sheltie's aptitude for work."

Even though the breed is moderate in size they have the heart of a lion and a strong instinct to protect their owners. Once I had a Sheltie wake me from a sound sleep in the middle of the night to warn me that someone was in our backyard. My husband was away so I let my dog out and called the police. My Sheltie followed the intruder with a little help from the wood pile we had stacked along the fence. She chased the intruder for blocks and cornered him holding him at bay until the police arrived.

Still another of my Shelties warded off a pack of wild dogs that were obviously intending to attack us while we were on a walk. My dog was outnumbered by far, but that meant nothing to him when his owner was faced with danger.

I feel as safe with a Sheltie as I would with the largest of breeds. A Sheltie would give his life to protect those he loves!

STANDARD of the Shetland Sheepdog

T he standard of the Shetland Sheepdog is well written in a straightforward manner that can be read and understood by even the beginning fancier. It must be understood, however, that it is only after many years of experience and observation that a person is really able to understand all the nuances of the breed. Reading as much as possible helps a great deal but nothing benefits the novice more than putting his or her self in the hands of a dedicated and experienced breeder.

Ch. Candega's Allies Elan Vital is an outstanding example of the beauty and grace that the Shetland Sheepdog should possess.

General Appearance— Preamble—The Shetland Sheepdog, like the Collie, traces to the Border Collie of Scotland, which, transported to the Shetland Islands and crossed with small intelligent, longhaired breeds, was reduced to miniature proportions. Subsequently crosses were made from time to time with Collies. This breed now bears the same relationship in size and general appearance to the Rough Collie as the Shetland Pony does to some of the larger breeds of horses. Although the resemblance between the Shetland Sheepdog and the Rough Collie is marked, there are differences which may be noted. The Shetland Sheepdog is a small, alert, rough-coated, longhaired working dog. He must be sound, agile and sturdy. The outline should be so symmetrical that no part appears out of proportion to the whole. Dogs should appear masculine; bitches feminine.

Size, Proportion, Substance—The Shetland Sheepdog should stand between 13 and 16 inches at the shoulder. Note: Height is determined by a line perpendicular to the ground

The Sheltie comes in a color for everyone. Tara Hill West Side Story owned by Ron and Bonnie Smith has a beautiful sable-colored coat.

from the top of the shoulder blades, the dog standing naturally, with forelegs parallel to the line of measurement.

Disqualifications—Heights below or above the desired size range are to be disqualified from the show ring.

In overall appearance, the body should appear moderately long as measured from the shoulder joint to ischium (rearmost extremity of the pelvic bone), but much of this length is actually due to the proper angulation and breadth of the shoulder and hindquarter, as the back itself should be comparatively short.

Head—The *head* should be refined and its shape, when viewed from top or side, be a long, blunt wedge tapering slightly from ears to nose.

The Sheltie's expression should be alert, intelligent, and gentle. K-9 Merlin owned by Denise Gustafson.

Expression—contours and chiseling of the head, the shape, set and use of ears, the placement, shape and color of the eyes combine to produce expression. Normally the expression should be alert, gentle, intelligent and questioning. Toward strangers the eyes should show watchfulness and reserve, but no fear.

Eyes medium size with dark, almond-shaped rims, set somewhat obliquely in skull. Color must be dark, with blue or merle eyes permissible in blue merles only. *Faults*—set too low. Hound, prick, bat, twisted ears. Leather too thick or too thin.

Skull and Muzzle—Top of skull should be flat, showing no prominence at nuchal crest (the top of the occiput). Cheeks should be flat and should merge smoothly into a well-rounded muzzle. Skull and muzzle should be of equal length, balance point being inner corner of eye. In profile the top line of skull should parallel the top line of muzzle, but on a higher plane due to the presence of a slight but definite stop. Jaws clean and powerful. The deep, well-developed underjaw, round at chin, should extend to base of nostril. *Nose* must be black. *Lips* tight. Upper and lower lips must meet and fit smoothly together all the way around. Teeth level and evenly spaced. Scissors *bite*.

Faults—Two-angled head. Too prominent stop, or no stop. Overfill below, between, or above eyes. Prominent nuchal crest. Domed skull. Prominent cheekbones. Snipy muzzle. Short, receding, or shallow underjaw, lacking breadth and depth. Overshot or undershot, missing or crooked teeth. Teeth visible when mouth is closed.

The Shetland Sheepdog should have a symmetrically proportioned body. Am. Can. Ch. Candega Moon Shadow owned by Daphne Allen.

Neck, Topline, Body—*Neck* should be muscular, arched, and of sufficient length to carry the head proudly. *Faults*—Too short and thick.

Back should be level and strongly muscled. *Chest* should be deep, the brisket reaching to point of elbow. The ribs should be well sprung, but flattened at their lower half to allow free play of the foreleg and shoulder. Abdomen moderately tucked up.

Faults—Back too long, too short, swayed or roached. Barrel ribs. Slab-side. Chest narrow and/or too shallow.

There should be a slight arch at the loins, and the *croup* should slope gradually to the rear. The hipbone (pelvis) should be set at a 30-degree angle to the spine. *Faults*—Croup higher than withers. Croup too straight or too steep.

The *tail* should be sufficiently long so that when it is laid along the back edge of the hind legs the last vertebra will reach the hock joint. Carriage of tail at rest is straight down or in a slight upward curve. When the dog is alert the tail is normally lifted, but it should not be curved forward over the back.

Faults—Too short. Twisted at end.

Forequarters—From the withers, the shoulder blades should slope at a 45-degree angle forward and downward to the shoulder joints. At the withers they are separated only by the vertebra, but they must slope outward sufficiently to accommodate the desired spring of rib. The upper arm should join the shoulder blade at as nearly as possible a right angle. Elbow joint should be equidistant from the ground or from the withers. Forelegs straight when viewed from all angles, muscular and clean, and of strong bone. Pasterns very strong, sinewy and flexible. Dewclaws may be removed. *Faults*— Insufficient angulation between shoulder and upper arm.

Ch. Hoodwink Nearly Neon is a striking example of a blue merle Shetland Sheepdog.

Upper arm too short. Lack of outward slope of shoulders. Loose shoulders. Turning in or out of elbows. Crooked legs. Light bone.

Feet should be oval and compact with the toes well arched and fitting tightly

The naturally athletic Sheltie has a smooth, free, and easy gait.

together. Pads deep and tough, nails hard and strong. *Faults*—Feet turning in or out. Splay feet. Hare feet. Cat feet.

Hindquarters—The thigh should be broad and muscular. The thighbone should be set into the pelvis at a right angle corresponding to the angle of the shoulder blade and upper arm. Stifle bones join the thighbone and should be distinctly angled at the stifle joint. The overall length of the stifle should at least equal the length of the thighbone, and preferably should slightly exceed it. Hock joint should be clean-cut, angular, sinewy, with good bone and strong ligamentation. The hock (metatarsus) should be short and straight when viewed from all angles. Dewclaws should be removed. *Faults*—Narrow thighs. Cow-hocks. Hocks turning out. Poorly defined hock joint.

Feet as in forequarters.

Coat—The coat should be double, the outer coat consisting of long, straight, harsh hair; the undercoat short, furry, and so dense as to give the entire coat its "standoff" quality. The hair on face, tips of ears and feet should be smooth. Mane and frill should be abundant, and particularly impressive in males. The forelegs well feathered, the hind legs heavily so, but smooth below the hock joint. Hair on tail profuse. *Note:* Excess hair on ears, feet, and on hocks may be trimmed for the show ring. *Faults*—Coat short or flat, in whole or in part; wavy, curly, soft or silky. Lack of undercoat. Smooth-coated specimens.

Ch. Trademark The Thunder Rolls is a nicely marked mahogany sable.

Color—Black, blue merle, and sable (ranging from golden through mahogany); marked with varying amount of white and/or tan. *Faults*—Rustiness in a black or blue coat. Washed-out or degenerate colors, such as pale sable and faded blue. Self-color in the case of blue merle, that is, without any merling or mottling and generally appearing as a faded or dilute tri-color. Conspicuous white body spots. Specimens with more than 50 percent white shall be so severely penalized as to effectively eliminate them from competition. *Disqualification*—Brindle.

Gait—The trotting gait of the Shetland Sheepdog should denote effortless speed and smoothness. There should be no jerkiness, nor stiff, stilted, up-and-down movement. The drive should be from the rear, true and straight, dependent upon correct angulation, musculation, and ligamentation of the entire hindquarter, thus allowing the dog to reach well under his body with his hind foot and propel himself forward. Reach of stride of the foreleg is dependent upon correct angulation, musculatation and ligamentation of the forequarters, together with correct width of chest and construction of rib cage. The foot should be lifted only enough to clear the ground as the leg swings forward. Viewed from the front, both forelegs and hindlegs should move forward almost perpendicular to ground

This young sable dog possesses the straight forelegs and eager expression of the Shetland Sheepdog.

at the walk, slanting a little inward at a slow trot, until at a swift trot the feet are brought so far inward toward center line at their inner edges. *There should be no crossing of the feet nor throwing of the weight from side to side.*

Faults—Stiff, short steps, with a choppy, jerky movement. Mincing steps, with a hopping up and down, or a balancing weight from side to side (often erroneously admired as a "dancing gait" but permissible in young puppies). Lifting of front feet in hackney-like action, resulting in loss of speed and energy. Pacing gait.

Temperament—The Shetland Sheepdog is intensely loyal, affectionate, and responsive to his owner. However, he may be reserved toward strangers but not to the point of showing fear or cringing in the ring. *Faults*—Shyness, timidity, or nervousness. Stubbornness, snippiness, or ill temper.

SELECTING the Right Shetland Sheepdog for You

WHAT TO LOOK FOR IN A BREEDER

Once the prospective Shetland Sheepdog owner satisfactorily finds all the answers to his or her questions relating to responsible ownership, he or she will undoubtedly want to rush out and purchase a puppy immediately. Take care—do not act in haste. It is extremely important for the buyer of any dog to do his homework. This is very important because it is not possible to ask a breeder the right questions if you know nothing about the breed. Read as much as you can. There are many breed specific and general care books available at local libraries and book stores.

The purchase of any dog is an important step since the well cared for dog will live with you for many years. In the case of a Shetland Sheepdog this could easily be 14 or perhaps even 15 or 16 years. You will undoubtedly want the dog you live with for that length of time to be one you will enjoy.

It is extremely important that your Sheltie be purchased from a breeder who has earned a reputation over the years for consistently producing dogs that are mentally and physically sound. There are always those who are ready and willing to exploit a breed for financial gain with no thought given to his health or welfare, or to the homes in which the dogs will be living.

Your Sheltie puppy will have a great start in life if his mother and father are healthy and well adjusted. If possible, meet the puppy's parents before taking him home.

The only way a breeder can earn a reputation for quality is through a well-thought-out breeding program in which rigid selectivity is imposed. Selective breeding is aimed at maintaining the virtues of a breed and eliminating genetic weaknesses. This process is time consuming and costly. Therefore, responsible Sheltie breeders protect their investment by providing the utmost in prenatal care for their brood matrons and maximum care

Make sure the breeder you are dealing with runs a quality facility and that the puppies are all healthy, clean, and well taken care of.

and nutrition for the resulting offspring. Once the puppies arrive, the knowledgeable breeder initiates a well-thought-out socialization process.

The socialization process is not one to be overlooked. It is what produces a mentally sound dog that will be able to live with people in harmony. Shetland Sheepdogs need human contact right from the beginning. It is important that the breeder spend a lot of time with each puppy individually in order to establish the human-canine relationship.

At Sandalwood we take each puppy away from his littermates at least once a day and rub each one's face against ours. This is done even before their eyes and ears have opened. We even carry them tied up in a sweatshirt close to our bodies. There is no better way to teach these puppies, however young, that human beings are their friends.

The first question a prospective owner should ask a breeder is, "What is the number one characteristic you breed for?" Deal only with those breeders that answer, "good temperament." Anything else is the first step on the road to tragedy.

The buyer should also ask what the breeder does with his or her Shelties. This will give some insight on the characteristics that a breeder is selecting for. No matter that a breeder is attempting to breed for outstanding show dogs. The responsible Sheltie breeder puts compatibility far ahead of any other characteristic. It will also tell the buyer which breeders actually live with their own dogs as pets—always a good sign.

The best puppies are born and raised in close proximity with their human family. At Sandalwood our puppies are kept close to us from the very beginning of their lives. They are imprinted with the *Play with the* scents and sounds of humans. Sheltie *Shetland Sheepdog* puppies that are born in a barn or *puppy you are* garage and that are given few *considering away* opportunities to be with humans *from his littermates.* seldom achieve their full potential as *A Hoodwink puppy* companions. *owned by Robin*

The buyer should look for cleanliness *Clemas.* in both the dogs and the areas in which the dogs are kept. Cleanliness is the first clue that tells you how much the breeder cares about the dogs he or she owns.

The governing kennel clubs in the different countries of the world maintain lists of local breed clubs and breeders that can lead a prospective dog buyer to responsible breeders of quality stock. Should you not be sure of where to contact a respected breeder in your area, we strongly recommend contacting your local kennel club for recommendations.

There is every possibility that a reputable breeder resides in your area who will not only be able to provide the right Sheltie for you but who will often have both parents of the puppy on the premises as well. This gives you an opportunity to see first hand what kind of dogs are in the background of the puppy you are considering. Good breeders are not only willing to have you see their dogs, but also to inspect the facility in which the dogs are raised as well. These breeders will also be able to discuss problems that exist in the breed with you and how they deal with these problems. Do not be surprised if a concerned breeder asks many questions about you and the environment in which your Sheltie will be raised. Good breeders are just as concerned with the quality of the homes to which their dogs are going as you are in obtaining a sound and healthy dog.

Do not think a good Sheltie puppy can only come from a large kennel. On the contrary, today many of the best breeders raise dogs in their homes as a hobby. It is important, however, that you not allow yourself to fall into the hands of an

irresponsible "backyard breeder." Backyard breeders separate themselves from the hobby breeder through their lack of responsibility to bring their breeding stock to its full potential. A hobby breeder's dogs find their way into the show and obedience ring or participating in the many and varied pursuits in which the Shetland Sheepdog excels. Quite simply, a backyard breeder is an individual who simply breeds dogs to sell.

If there are no local breeders in your area, there are legitimate and reliable breeders throughout the country that will appear on the Shetland Sheepdog Club or national kennel club lists. These established breeders are accustomed to safely shipping puppies to different states, even different countries.

Always check references of these breeders and do not hesitate to ask for documentation of their answers. The breeder will undoubtedly have as many questions for you as you will have for him or her. When you call a far away breeder, call at a reasonable hour, and expect to have a lengthy conversation. The amount of money you invest in a satisfying telephone conversation may save you huge veterinary costs and a great deal of unhappiness.

HEALTH CONCERNS

All breeds of dogs have genetic problems that must be paid attention to and just because a male and female do not have evidence of problems, this does not mean their pedigrees are free of something that might be entirely incapacitating. Again, rely upon recommendations from national kennel clubs or local breed clubs when looking for a breeder.

A Shetland Sheepdog puppy needs a good-quality nutritious dog food formulated for growth.

Breed health problems can only be eliminated by thoughtful breeders who are willing to breed selectively and discuss these issues openly. It is important that you ask the breeder you are considering about the following:

Hip Dysplasia—a degenerative deformity of the hip joint which causes lameness and in advanced cases, extreme pain.

Von Willebrand's Disease—a disease affecting blood coagulation.

Your Sheltie can pick up parasites from the outdoors and from other dogs. Make sure your dog is properly vaccinated before you let him outside.

A Sheltie puppy is very vulnerable and needs to be examined by a veterinarian as soon as you acquire him.

Eye Problems—Shelties can be affected with numerous eye problems including: Progressive retinal

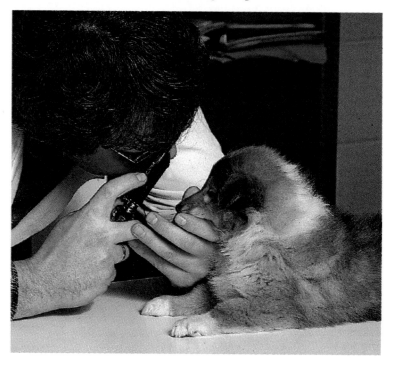

atrophy, cataracts, ectasia syndrome (a retinal vessel problem) and trichiasis.

Thyroid deficiency.

Deafness—it is extremely important to check the hearing of white and double merle puppies in particular.

Take your Sheltie wherever you go—there is nothing better for him!

Nowadays, many breeders are also certifying elbows and thyroid function with the Orthopedic Foundation for Animals (OFA). Again, it is important that both the buyer and the seller ask questions. This is not to say the puppy you buy or his relatives will be afflicted with any of the above, but concerned breeders are well aware of their presence in the breed.

The concerned breeder uses all the answers you give to match the right puppy with the right home. Households with boisterous children generally need a puppy that differs from the one appropriate for a sedate, single adult. The time you spend in making the right selection insures you of getting the right Sheltie for your lifestyle.

If questions are not asked, information is not received. We would be highly suspect of a person who is willing to sell you a Sheltie with "no questions asked."

RECOGNIZING A HEALTHY PUPPY

Most breeders do not release their puppies until the puppies have been given their "puppy shots." Normally, this is at about seven to nine weeks of age. At this age they will bond extremely well with their new owners and the puppies are entirely weaned.

Nursing puppies receive temporary immunization from their mother. Once weaned, however, a

Properly socialization is the key to a well-behaved Sheltie.

A Shetland Sheepdog may seem like the perfect gift, but make sure the receiver is ready to accept the responsibility of dog ownership.

puppy is highly susceptible to many infectious diseases that can be transmitted via the hands and clothing of people. Therefore, it behooves you to make sure your puppy is fully inoculated before he leaves his home environment, and to know when any additional inoculations should be given.

Above all, the Sheltie puppy you buy should be a happy, bouncy, extrovert. The worst thing you could possibly do is buy a shy, shrinking-violet puppy, or one that appears sick and listless because you feel sorry for him. Doing this will undoubtedly lead to heartache and difficulty to say nothing of the veterinary costs that you may incur in getting the puppy well.

If at all possible take the puppy you are interested in away from his littermates into another room or another part of the kennel. The smells will remain the same for the puppy so he should still feel secure and maintain his outgoing personality but it will give you an opportunity to inspect the puppy more closely. A healthy little Sheltie puppy will be strong and sturdy to the touch, never bony, or on the other hand, obese and bloated. The inside of the puppy's ears should be pink and clean. Dark discharge or a bad odor could indicate ear mites, a sure sign of poor maintenance. The healthy Sheltie puppy's breath smells sweet. The teeth are clean and white and there should never be any malformation of the mouth or jaw. The puppy's eyes should be clear and bright. Eyes that appear runny and irritated indicate serious problems.

To ensure against genetic diseases and to preserve the quality of their programs, reputable breeders will screen all Shelties before breeding them.

There should be no sign of discharge from the nose, nor should it be crusted or runny. Coughing or diarrhea are danger signals, as are any eruptions on the skin. The coat should be soft and lustrous.

The healthy Sheltie puppy's front legs should be straight as little posts and the movement light and bouncy. The best way to describe a Sheltie puppy's movement is like that of a mechanical wind-up toy with legs that cover considerable ground. Of course there is always a chubby, clumsy puppy or two in a litter. Do not mistake this for unsoundness but if ever you have any doubts, discuss them with the breeder.

Remember, your choice will be living with you for a long time. Make sure the puppy reacts well to you. Run your fingers along the ground and see if the puppy is willing to play. If the puppy has no interest in you and the only thing he seems to have interest in is getting back to his littermates, definitely choose another puppy.

MALE OR FEMALE?

If you have decided upon the sex of the puppy you want, do not let a breeder try to change your mind because that sex is not available. If you want a male, buy a male. This is one breed where there aren't a great deal of sex-related differences.

Actually the biggest difference is in coat. The mature male's coat is far more luxurious (and therefore requires more care for its upkeep). This can be compared to the growth pattern in lions—the hair is much longer and much thicker around the neck, shoulders and chest of the male.

Females have their semiannual heat cycles once they have passed nine or ten months of age. During these heat cycles of approximately 21 days, the female must be confined to avoid soiling her surroundings with the bloody discharge that accompanies estrus. She must also be carefully watched to prevent males from gaining access to her or she will become pregnant.

While owners of other breeds find training males not to "lift their leg" and mark their territory indoors troublesome, most Sheltie males are not difficult to correct in this respect. Unless the dog has a highly developed herding instinct, Sheltie males seldom go wandering. They are far more interested in staying home to watch over their families.

It should be understood that most sexually related problems can be avoided by having the pet Shetland Sheepdog "altered." Spaying the female and neutering the male saves the pet owner all the headaches of either of the sexually related problems, without changing the character of the breed. If there is any

The puppies you are considering should be bright-eyed, healthy, and happy. These ten-week-old pups from September Shelties are ready for a new home.

change at all in the altered Shetland Sheepdog it is in making the dog an even more amiable companion. Above all, altering your pet precludes the possibility of him adding to the serious pet overpopulation problems that exist worldwide.

Good temperament is passed down from parents to offspring.

SELECTING A SHOW PROSPECT PUPPY

It should be understood that the most any breeder can offer is an opinion on the "show potential" of a particular puppy. The most promising eight-week-old puppy can grow up to be a mediocre adult. A breeder has no control over this.

Any predictions breeders make about a puppy's future are based upon their experience with past litters

Socialization with people is very important for your Sheltie puppy's well being. A well-socialized puppy will get along with anyone.

45

which have produced winning show dogs. It is obvious that the more successful a breeder has been in producing winning Shetland Sheepdogs over the years, the broader his or her base of comparison will be.

A puppy's potential as a show dog is determined by how closely he adheres to the demands of the standard of the breed. While most breeders concur there is no such thing as "a sure thing" when it comes to predicting winners, they are also quick to agree that the older a puppy is, the better your chances are of making any predictions at all.

It makes little difference to the owner of a pet if his Sheltie is badly marked or if an ear hangs down a bit. Neither would it make a difference if a male pup has only one testicle. These faults do not interfere with a Sheltie becoming a healthy, loving companion. However, these flaws would keep that Sheltie from a winning show career.

It's a big world out there for your little puppy, and he will need your guidance and discipline. Eight-week-old Sandalwood's Wet 'n Wild owned by Linda and Rick

While it certainly behooves the prospective buyer of a show prospect puppy to be as familiar with the standard of the breed as possible, it is even more important for the buyer to put his or herself into the hands of a successful and respected breeder of winning Shelties. The experienced breeder knows there are certain age-related shortcomings in young Shetland Sheepdogs that maturity will take care of, and other faults that completely eliminate it from consideration as a show prospect. Also, breeders are always looking for the right homes in which to place their show prospect puppies and will be particularly helpful in this respect when they know you plan to show one of their dogs.

All puppies go through an awkward stage, but your Sheltie pup should look a lot like his parents, only smaller.

The important thing to remember in choosing your first show prospect is "cuteness" may not be consistent with quality. An extroverted puppy in the litter might decide he belongs to you. If you are simply looking for a pet, that is the puppy for you. However, if you are genuinely interested in showing your Sheltie, you must keep your head and, without disregarding good temperament, give serious consideration to what the standard says a show-type Sheltie must be.

The complete standard of the breed is presented in this book and its content is what, in the end, determines the show potential of a puppy. When we are selecting a show-quality puppy, all the foregoing regarding soundness and health apply here as well. A point to remember, however, is that spaying and castration are not reversible procedures and once done eliminate the possibility of ever breeding or showing your Sheltie in conformation shows. Altered dogs can, however, be shown in obedience and herding trials and many other competitive events.

There are a good number of additional points to be considered for the show dog as well. When we are selecting a show-quality puppy we are looking for overall balance and that "look at me attitude" that is so important in the show ring. A show dog is put under a lot more stress than a companion dog that spends his days at home. It is important that the show dog be able to hold up under the stress that will be created by sometimes constant travel.

It is also very important that the puppy be within the size limits for the age of the dog. Without exception the adult Sheltie must measure between 13 and 16 inches at the highest point of the shoulder. Anything over or under those limits is a disqualification and the dog cannot be shown. We have charted the size of every puppy we have ever raised. Now, because of past experience we can get pretty close to predicting what the full height of the dog will be as an adult. Because of the variety of breeds in the Shetland Sheepdog's background, ranging from Pomeranian to standard sized Collie, there is always that element of chance in determining size.

Even in an eight-week-old puppy, we expect to see good movement and soundness which are of paramount importance when judging this working breed. The dogs have to be sturdy but moderate in bone, but above all agile in order to perform as stock dogs. Structure is the main area of concern and we at Sandalwood make no concessions in that area.

Puppy Or Adult?

A young puppy is not your only option when contemplating the purchase of a Sheltie. In some cases an adult dog or older puppy may be just the answer. It certainly eliminates the trials and tribulations of housebreaking, chewing, and the myriad of other problems associated with a very young puppy. Inoculations become a once-a-year thing instead of the frequent puppy shots. Very often the adult Sheltie will be already spayed or neutered.

There are also some disadvantages that might have to be overcome. Shelties are very bonded to their owners. The adjustment period necessary for this to take place with a new owner may be considerably longer with a mature dog than it might be for a very young puppy. A little extra attention can help a great deal in this respect.

A few adult Shelties may have become set in their ways and while you may not have to contend with the problems of puppyhood, do realize there is the occasional adult that may have developed habits that do not entirely suit you or your lifestyle. Arrange to bring an adult Sheltie into your home on a trial basis. That way neither you nor the dog will be obligated should either of you decide you are incompatible.

IMPORTANT PAPERS

The purchase of any purebred dog entitles you to three very important documents: a health record containing an inoculation list, a copy of the dog's pedigree and a registration certificate.

Health Record: Most Shetland Sheepdog breeders have initiated the necessary inoculation series for their puppies by the time they are eight weeks of age. These inoculations protect the puppies against hepatitis, leptospirosis, distemper, and canine parvovirus. In most cases, rabies inoculations are not given until a puppy is four months of age or older.

There is a set series of inoculations developed to combat these infectious diseases and it is extremely important that you obtain a record of the shots your puppy has been given and the

Puppies are full of endless energy and need constant supervision, as well as a lot of rest. Hoodwink Endless Winter owned by Terry Smith takes a well-deserved nap.

dates upon which the shots were administered. In this way the veterinarian you choose will be able to continue on with the appropriate inoculation series as needed.

Pedigree: The pedigree is your dog's "family tree." The breeder must supply you with a copy of this document authenticating your puppy's ancestors back to at least the third generation. All purebred dogs have a pedigree. The pedigree does not imply that a dog is of show quality. It is simply a chronological list of ancestors.

A lot of love and surprises in a tiny package—that's what is in store for a new Sheltie owner.

Registration Certificate: The registration certificate is the canine world's "birth certificate." This certificate is issued by a country's governing kennel club. When you transfer the ownership of your Sheltie from the breeder's name to your own name, the transaction is entered on this certificate and once mailed to the kennel club, it is permanently recorded in their computerized files. Keep all these documents in a safe place as you will need them when you visit your veterinarian or should you ever wish to breed or show your Sheltie.

DIET SHEET

Your Sheltie is the happy healthy puppy he is because the breeder has been carefully feeding and caring for him. Every breeder we know has their own particular way of doing this. Most breeders give the new owner a written record that details the amount and kind of food a puppy has been receiving. Do follow these recommendations to the letter at least for the first month or two after the puppy comes to live with you.

The diet sheet should indicate the number of times a day your puppy has been accustomed to being fed and the kind of vitamin supplementation, if any, he has been receiving. Following the prescribed procedure will reduce the chance of upset stomach and loose stools.

It is easy to fall in love with an adorable Shetland Sheepdog puppy. Tara Hill Fantasia owned by Bonnie Smith.

Usually a breeder's diet sheet projects the increases and changes in food that will be necessary as your puppy grows from week to week. If the sheet does not include this information ask the breeder for suggestions regarding increases and the eventual changeover to adult food.

In the unlikely event you are not supplied with a diet sheet by the breeder and are unable to get one, your veterinarian will be able to advise you in this respect. There are countless foods now being manufactured expressly to meet the nutritional needs of puppies and growing dogs. A trip down the pet aisle at your local pet supply store will prove just how many choices you have. Two important tips: read labels carefully for content, and when dealing with established, reliable manufacturers remember that you are more likely to get what you pay for.

HEALTH GUARANTEE

Any reputable breeder is more than willing to supply a written agreement that the sale of your Sheltie is contingent upon several things. Although all are equally important, certainly the puppy must be able to pass a veterinarian's examination. Further, the puppy should be guaranteed against the development of any hereditary problems. Last, but not least, the

The breeder will have started your Sheltie pup on the road to good nutrition, so stick to this original diet when you first bring him home.

Pet ownership can teach a child responsibility and respect for animals. Heather and her Sheltie friend Tad are perfect playmates.

temperament of the puppy you purchase should be vouched for. There is a period of adjustment all puppies go through when they first go to a new home, but that should be relatively short.

Ideally you will be able to arrange an appointment with your chosen veterinarian right after you have picked up your puppy from the breeder and before you take the puppy home. If this is not possible you should not delay this procedure any longer than 24 hours from the time you take your puppy home.

TEMPERAMENT AND SOCIALIZATION

Temperament is both hereditary and learned. Inherited good temperament can be ruined by poor treatment and lack of proper socialization. A Shetland Sheepdog puppy that has inherited a bad temperament is a poor risk as a companion, a show dog, or a working dog and should certainly never be bred from. Therefore, it is critical that you obtain a happy puppy from a breeder who is determined to produce good

Take your Sheltie pups with you wherever you go. The more people your Sheltie meets, the better socialized he will become.

temperaments and has taken all the necessary steps to provide the early socialization necessary.

It is important to remember a Sheltie puppy may be as happy as a lark living at home with you and your family but if the socialization begun by the breeder is not continued, that sunny disposition will not extend outside your front door. From the day the young Sheltie arrives at your home, you must be committed to accompanying it upon an unending pilgrimage to meet and like all human beings and animals.

If you are fortunate enough to have children well past the toddler stage in the household or living nearby, your socialization task will be assisted considerably. Shetland Sheepdogs raised with children seem to have a distinct advantage in socialization. The two seem to understand each other and in some way, known only to the puppies and children themselves, they give each other the confidence to face the trying ordeal of growing up.

The children in your own household are not the only children your puppy should spend time with. It is a case of the more the merrier! Every child (and adult for that matter) that enters your household should be asked to pet your puppy.

It is important that Sheltie puppies have time to play with their littermates in order to learn how to interact with other dogs later in life.

Your puppy should go everywhere with you: the post office, the market, to the shopping mall—wherever. Little Sheltie puppies create a stir wherever they go and dog lovers will want to stop and pet the puppy. There is nothing in the world better for the puppy. They are social dogs by nature.

The breed standard calls for the Shetland Sheepdog's temperament to be reserved towards strangers, but not to the point of shyness. There is a certain degree of caution in a Sheltie's attitude toward strangers, but a Sheltie should never run and hide from people he doesn't know. A Sheltie with a confident attitude may well stand back and bark at someone he doesn't know, but a mentally sound Shetland Sheepdog is never a coward.

If your Sheltie has a show career in his future, there are other things in addition to just being handled that will have to be taught. All show dogs must learn to have their mouths opened and inspected by the judge. The judge must be able to check the teeth. Males must be accustomed to having their testicles touched as the dog show judge must determine that all male dogs are "complete," which means there are two normal sized testicles in the scrotum. These inspections must begin in puppyhood and be done on a regular and continuing basis.

All Shelties must learn to get along well with other dogs as well as with humans. If you are fortunate enough to have a "puppy preschool" or dog training class near-by, attend with as much regularity as you possibly can. A young Sheltie that has been exposed regularly to other dogs from puppyhood will learn to adapt and accept other dogs and other breeds much more readily than one that seldom sees strange dogs.

THE ADOLESCENT SHETLAND SHEEPDOG

You will find it amazing how quickly the little ball of fur you first brought home begins to develop into a full grown Shetland Sheepdog. Some lines shoot up to full size very rapidly, others mature more slowly. Some Shelties pass through adolescence quite gracefully, but most grow out of their puppy fluff and become lanky and ungainly growing in and out of proportion seemingly from one day to the next.

Food needs usually increase during this growth period. However, some Shelties seem as if they can never get enough to eat, while others experience a very finicky stage in their eating habits and seem to eat enough only to keep from starving. Think of Sheltie puppies as individualistic as children and act accordingly.

The amount of food you give your Sheltie should be adjusted to how much he will readily consume at each meal. If the entire meal is eaten quickly, add a small amount more to the next feeding and continue to do so as the need increases. This method will insure you of giving your puppy enough food. You must also pay close attention to the dog's appearance and conditions, as you do not want a Sheltie puppy to become overweight or obese.

At eight weeks of age a Sheltie puppy is eating four meals a day. By the time the puppy is four months old the puppy can do well on two meals a day, fed morning and evening, with perhaps a snack in the middle of the day. If your puppy does not eat the food offered, it is either not hungry or not well. Your dog will eat when he is hungry. If you suspect the dog is not well, a trip to the veterinarian is in order.

After the dog is a year old we feed once a day just before we eat our own dinner. In this way a trip outdoors just before bedtime will usually ensure the dog spending an accident-free night.

Many dog owners feel their dogs need far more food than what they actually require. Overfeeding is very harmful to their bodies. It puts stress on their kidneys and heart. It can also make them very lazy, which in turn will cause them to gain even more weight from lack of exercise.

Feeding a diet too high in protein can be very harmful to the Shetland Sheepdog because it can lead to "hot spots" (eruptions in the skin). Remember a Sheltie is a long haired breed and that coat keeps their bodies well insulated. Protein creates heat and too much leads to skin problems.

This adolescent period is a particularly important and sometimes difficult one. Hormones are developing and it can have an effect on the temperament of the dog. Boy puppies realize they are males and may test their ability to dominate. The girls tend to get silly. This is also the time your Sheltie must learn all the household and social rules that he will live with for the rest of his life. Your patience and commitment during this difficult time will not only produce a respected canine good citizen, but will forge a bond between the two of you that will grow and ripen into a wonderful relationship.

The adolescent Sheltie needs patience and training in order to become a valued family member and a well-behaved pet.

CARING for Your Shetland Sheepdog

The best way to make sure your Sheltie puppy is obtaining the right amount and the correct type of food for his age is to follow the diet sheet provided by the breeder from whom you obtain your puppy. Do your best not to change the puppy's diet and you will be less apt to run into digestive problems and diarrhea. Diarrhea is very serious in young puppies. Puppies with diarrhea can dehydrate very rapidly causing severe problems and even death.

If it is necessary to change your puppy's diet for any reason it should never be done abruptly. Begin by adding a tablespoon or two of the new food, gradually increasing the amount until the meal consists entirely of the new product. A rule of thumb is this: you should be able to feel the ribs and backbone with just a slight layer of fat and muscle over them.

Over feeding is very harmful to the Shetland Sheepdog. It puts stress on the kidneys and heart. It also can make a Sheltie very lazy and disinterested in the exercise necessary to keep the breed in shape.

By the time your Sheltie puppy is 12 months old you can reduce feedings to one a day. This meal can be given either in the morning or evening. It is really a matter of choice on your part. There are two important things to remember; feed the main meal at the same time every day, and make sure what you feed is nutritionally complete.

If you wish, the single meal can be cut in half and fed twice a day. A morning or night time snack of hard dog biscuits made especially for medium dogs can also be given. These biscuits not only become highly anticipated treats, but are genuinely helpful in maintaining healthy gums and teeth.

"Balanced" Diets: In order for a canine diet to qualify as "complete and balanced" in the United States, it must meet standards set by the Subcommittee on Canine Nutrition of the National Research Council of the National Academy of Sciences. Most commercial foods manufactured for dogs meet these standards and prove this by listing the ingredients contained in the food on every package and can. The ingredients are listed in descending order with the main ingredient listed first.

Fed with any regularity at all, refined sugars can cause your Shetland Sheepdog to become obese, and will definitely create tooth decay. Refined sugars are not a part of the canine natural food acquisition and canine teeth are not genetically disposed to handling these sugars. Do not feed your Sheltie sugar products and avoid products that contain sugar to any high degree.

A puppy receives his first nutrients from his mother. After he is weaned, it is up to you, his owner, to provide your Sheltie with the proper diet.

Fresh water and a properly prepared, balanced diet, containing the essential nutrients in correct proportions are all a healthy Shetland Sheepdog needs to be offered. Dog foods come canned, dry, semi-moist, "scientifically fortified," and "all-natural." A visit to your local market or pet store will reveal how vast an array you will be able to select from.

The important thing to remember is that all dogs, whether they are Shetland Sheepdogs, Collies, or Cocker Spaniels, are carnivorous (meat-eating) animals. While the vegetable content of your dog's diet should not be overlooked, a dog's physiology and anatomy are based upon carnivorous food acquisition. Animal protein and fats are essential to the well being of your Sheltie. However, a diet too high in proteins can lead to problems as well. Not all dry foods contain the proper amount of protein that will keep the healthy Shetland Sheepdog in top condition. It is best to discuss this with the breeder from whom you purchase your dog or with your veterinarian.

It should also be realized that in the wild carnivores eat practically the entire beast they capture and kill. The carnivore's kills consist almost entirely of herbivore (plant eating) animals and invariably the carnivore begins his meal with the contents of the herbivore's stomach. This provides the carbohydrates, minerals and nutrients present in vegetables.

Through centuries of domestication we have made our dogs entirely dependent upon us for their well being. Therefore we, as owners, are completely responsible for duplicating the food balance the wild dog finds in nature. The domesticated dog's diet must include protein, carbohydrates, fats, roughage and small amounts of essential minerals and vitamins.

Pick a good quality dog food that is nutritionally adequate and appropriate for your Shetland Sheepdog's stage of life.

Finding commercially prepared diets that contain all the necessary nutrients will not present a problem. It is important to understand though that these commercially prepared foods do contain all the necessary nutrients your Sheltie needs. It is therefore unnecessary to add vitamin supplements to these diets in other than special circumstances prescribed by your veterinarian. These "special periods in a Sheltie's life can include the time of rapid growth the breed experiences in puppyhood, the female's pregnancy, and the time during which she is nursing her puppies.

Even when required in these special circumstances it is not a case of "if a little is good, more is better." Over-supplementation and forced growth are now looked upon by some breeders as major contributors to many skeletal abnormalities found in the purebred dogs of the day.

Over-supplementation: A great deal of controversy exists today regarding the orthopedic

It is fine to give your Sheltie occasional treats as long as they are nutritious and do not upset his regular diet.

problems that afflict some Shetland Sheepdogs and many other breeds. Some claim these problems and a wide variety of chronic skin conditions are entirely hereditary, but many others feel they can be exacerbated by diet and over-use of mineral and vitamin supplements for puppies.

In giving vitamin supplementation one should never exceed the prescribed amount. Some breeders insist all recommended dosages be halved before including them in a dog's diet because of the highly fortified commercial foods being fed. Still other breeders feel no supplementation should be given at all, believing a balanced diet that includes plenty of milk products and a small amount of bone meal to provide calcium is all that is necessary and beneficial.

If the owner of a Shetland Sheepdog normally eats healthy nutritious food, there is no reason why his dog cannot be given table scraps. Table scraps, however, should be given only as part of the dog's meal and never from the table. A Sheltie that becomes accustomed to being hand fed from

The POPpup™ is a healthy treat for your Sheltie. Its bone-hard consistency helps control plaque. When microwaved, it becomes a rich cracker your Sheltie will love. The POPpup™ is available in many flavors and is fortified with calcium.

the table can become a real pest at meal time very quickly. Also, dinner guests may find the pleading stare of your Sheltie less than appealing when dinner is being served.

Dogs do not care if food looks like a hot dog or wedge of cheese. Truly nutritious dog foods are seldom manufactured to look like food that appeals to humans. Dogs only care about how food smells and tastes. It is highly doubtful you will be eating your dog's food so do not waste your money on these "looks just like" products.

Along these lines, most of the moist foods or canned foods that have the look of "delicious red beef" look that way because they contain great amounts of preservatives, sugars, and dyes. These additives are no better for your dog than they are for you.

Special Diets: There are now any number of commercially prepared diets for dogs with special dietary needs. The overweight, underweight, or geriatric dog can have his nutritional needs met as can puppies and growing dogs. The calorie

Make sure your Shetland Sheepdog has plenty of cool clean water available to him at all times.

content of these foods is adjusted accordingly. With the correct amount of the right foods and the proper amount of exercise, your Sheltie should stay in top shape. Common sense must prevail. What works for humans works for dogs as well—increasing calories will increase weight; stepping up exercise, and reducing calories will bring weight down.

Occasionally a young Shetland Sheepdog going through the teething period will become a finicky eater. The concerned owner's first response is to tempt the dog by hand-feeding special treats and foods that the problem eater seems to prefer. This practice only serves to compound the problem. Once the dog learns to play the waiting game, he will turn up his nose at anything other than his favorite food knowing full well what he wants to eat will eventually arrive. Give your Sheltie the proper food you want him to eat. The dog may well turn up his nose a day or two and refuse to eat anything. However, you can rest assured when your dog is really hungry he will eat.

Unlike humans, dogs have no suicidal tendencies. A healthy dog will not starve himself to death. He may not eat enough to keep himself in the shape we find ideal and attractive but he will definitely eat enough to maintain himself. If your Sheltie is not eating properly and appears to be too thin, it is probably best to consult your veterinarian.

BATHING AND GROOMING

The Shetland Sheepdog is a natural breed that requires no clipping or trimming. This does not mean the breed needs no coat care at all. Regular thorough brushing, and a bath, when needed, are an important part of keeping your dog clean, healthy and a pleasant companion.

Because shampoo residue can cause skin irritation, be sure to rinse his coat thoroughly when you bathe your Sheltie.

Many people think a Sheltie's coat is hard to manage. This need not be true. The male dog will shed twice a year—once in the summer and once around his birthday. The female will shed just after being in heat or if she has been spayed, when she would normally have been in heat. Brushing is of course, important at this time.

The rest of the year, although there will always be a few hairs around, the amount is minimal. No more than what a human leaves in his comb or brush.

The nice thing about the Sheltie's hair is that it does not burrow into the sofa or clothing. It can be taken up with your hand with little or no difficulty.

There is a tendency for people to bathe their Shelties too often. Do not give your Sheltie a bath unless he begins to smell foul. You can freshen up the coat by sprinkling a little baby powder on it and then working it in well. This also makes the dog smell very good.

The Sheltie's luxurious coat needs regular grooming. If you accustom your dog to these procedures early, he will come to enjoy the time you spend together.

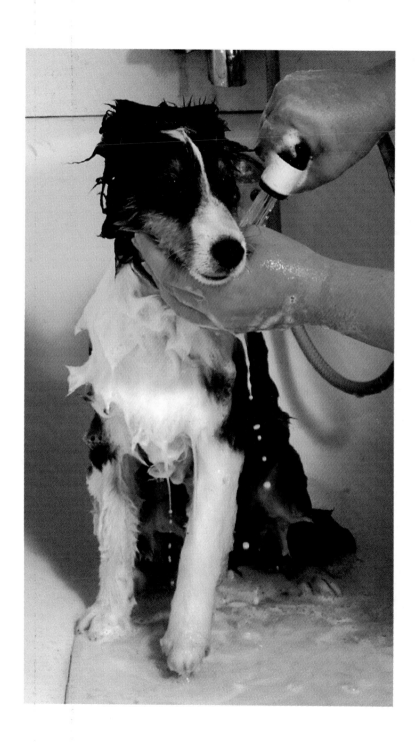

This procedure can even help if the dog has gotten into the mud and you do not have time to give him a bath. Wait until the mud dries, sprinkle in the baby powder and then brush it out. It really cleans and also gives an amazing sparkle to the white areas of the coat.

Overbathing can lead to dry skin problems. Dry skin creates a need to scratch and this can lead to severe scratching and "hot spots"—moist sore areas in which the coat is entirely scratched away.

The easiest way to groom a Sheltie is by placing him on a grooming table. A grooming table can be built or purchased at your local pet shop. Make sure the table is of a height at which you can work comfortably either sitting or standing. Adjustable-height grooming tables are available at most pet outlets.

Although you will buy the grooming table when your puppy first arrives, anticipate your dog's full grown size in making your purchase and select or build a table that will accommodate a fully grown Sheltie. It is best to use a grooming table that has an "arm" and a "noose." The noose slips around the dog's neck when he is standing and keeps the dog from fidgeting about or deciding he has had enough grooming.

You will need to invest in two brushes: a "pin" brush that has long wire bristles set in rubber for the long hair, and a "slicker" brush that has shorter, angled bristles is best used on the shorter hair of the head and feet and to help break up mats that may occur. You will also need a steel comb to remove any debris that collects in the longer furnishings. A comb that has teeth divided between fine and coarse is ideal. Consider the

Grooming is a great way to inspect the condition of your dog's skin and coat and keep on top of any health problems he may have.

fact that you will be using this equipment for many years so buy the best of these items that you can afford.

Any attempt to groom your puppy on the floor may result in you spending a good part of your time chasing him around the room. Nor is sitting on the floor for long stretches of time the most comfortable position in the world for the average adult.

Good oral hygiene is important to the overall health of your Shetland Sheepdog.

Brush drying your Sheltie's coat with the assistance of a hair dryer will reduce drying time significantly.

Teaching your Sheltie to lie on his side on the grooming table can make your grooming chores infinitely easier. Once taught to do so, many Shelties become so relaxed during their grooming sessions they may fall sound asleep.

When brushing, go through the coat from the skin out. Do this all over the body and be especially careful to attend to the hard-to-reach areas between the legs, behind the ears, and under the body. While the correct Shetland Sheepdog coat seldom mats or tangles, this may occur during the time when the Sheltie is shedding his puppy coat or if an adult catches burrs or sticky substances in his longer furnishings.

A gentle introduction to grooming procedures at an early age will make the experience pleasurable for both you and your Sheltie.

Should you encounter a mat that does not brush out, easily use your fingers and the steel comb to separate the hairs as much as possible. Do not cut or pull out the matted hair. Apply baby powder or one of the specially prepared grooming powders directly to the mat and brush completely from the skin out.

Nail Trimming: This is a good time to accustom your Sheltie to having his nails trimmed and having his feet inspected. Your puppy may not particularly like this part of his toilette, but with patience and the passing of time he will eventually resign himself to the fact that these "manicures" are a part of life. Nail trimming must be done with care in that it is important not to cut into the "quick." Dark nails make it difficult to see the quick that grows close to the end of the nail and contains very sensitive nerve endings. If the nail is allowed to grow too long it will be impossible to cut it back to a proper length without cutting into the quick. This causes severe pain to the dog and can also result in a great deal of bleeding that can be very difficult to stop.

The nails of a Sheltie who

Shelties require some vegetable matter in their diet. The Carrot Bone ™ by Nylabone® fights plaque, satisfies their desire to chew, and is nutritious. It is highly recommended as a healthy toy for your Sheltie.

spends most of his time indoors or on grass when outdoors can grow long very quickly. Do not allow the nails to become overgrown and then expect to cut them back easily. If your Sheltie is getting plenty of exercise on cement or rough hard pavement, the nails may keep sufficiently worn down. Otherwise they must then be carefully trimmed back.

Should the quick be nipped in the trimming process, there are any number of blood clotting products available at pet shops that will almost immediately stem the flow of blood. It is wise to have one of these products on hand in case there is a nail trimming accident or the dog tears a nail on his own.

There are coarse metal files available at your local pet shop that can be used in place of the nail clippers. This is a more gradual method of taking the nail back and one is far less apt to injure the quick.

The Wet Bath: Consistent brushing and a wash cloth will keep the Sheltie's coat surprisingly clean but there are occasions where a full bath may be required. Following the foregoing coat care procedure will all but eliminate the need for bathing a Shetland Sheepdog more than a few times during the year.

On the occasion your Sheltie requires a wet bath you will need to gather the necessary equipment ahead of time. A rubber mat should be placed at the bottom of the tub to avoid your dog slipping and thereby becoming frightened. A rubber spray hose is absolutely necessary to remove all shampoo residue.

A small cotton ball placed inside each ear will avoid water running down into the dog's ear canal. Be very careful when washing around the eyes as soaps and shampoos can be extremely irritating. A tiny dab of petroleum jelly or a drop of mineral oil in each eye will help prevent shampoo irritating the eye.

In bathing, start behind the ears and work back.

A Sheltie's feet must be inspected regularly for injuries and his toenails kept short to prevent any tearing or discomfort.

Your Shetland Sheepdog must become accustomed to extensive grooming if he is to be shown in conformation.

Use a wash cloth to soap and rinse around the head and face. Once you have shampooed your dog, you must rinse the coat thoroughly and when you feel quite certain all shampoo residue has been removed, rinse once more. Shampoo residue in the coat is sure to dry the hair and cause skin irritation.

As soon as you have completed the bath use heavy towels to remove as much of the excess water as possible. Your Sheltie will undoubtedly assist you in the process by shaking a great deal of the water out of his coat on his own.

Brush drying the coat with the assistance of a hair dryer (human or special canine blower-type) will reduce drying time significantly. When using a hair dryer of any kind, always keep the setting on "medium." Anything warmer can dry the coat and in extreme cases actually burn the skin. Do not blow directly into the coat but over it and use your brush to fluff out the hair and assist the drying process.

EXERCISE

Sufficient exercise is just good sense. Remember the breed's heritage—the Shetland Sheepdog was bred to work a full day, every day!

Needless to say puppies should never be forced to exercise. Normally, they are little dynamos of energy and keep themselves busy all day long interspersed with frequent naps.

Shelties need a safe haven from the elements and a place to call their own. Provide adequate shelter for your Sheltie if he is to be outside for long periods of time.

Mature Shelties are not only capable, they are delighted to be jogging companions. It is important, however, to use good judgment in any exercise program. Begin slowly and increase the distance to be covered very gradually over an extended period of time. Use special precautions in hot weather. High temperatures and forced exercise are a dangerous combination.

If confined to a small area, like a crate, too long, some Shelties will repeatedly turn circles when they become excited. This is not because a Sheltie is hyper or high strung, it is a natural herding instinct manifesting itself. A Sheltie moves from side to side when he herds a flock of sheep and if restricted from doing this he is inclined to turn all the way around instead.

The best exercise for a Shetland Sheepdog, however, is that which it acquires in the pursuit of the many organized activities for which the breed is particularly well suited. Agility, flyball, obedience, and herding activities exercise the Sheltie's mind and his body. There is no better way to insure your Sheltie of a happy, healthy existence.

SOCIALIZATION

It should be understood that a young dog that has never been exposed to strangers, traffic noises, or boisterous children could become confused and frightened. It is important that a Sheltie owner give his or her dog the opportunity to experience all of these situations gradually and with his trusted owner present for support.

Shelties are good natured and happy dogs in general and very pleasant to be around. They are social dogs by nature. Although the breed standard calls for the Shetland Sheepdog temperament to be reserved toward strangers, this is not to be confused with shyness or timidity.

HOUSEBREAKING and Training Your Shetland Sheepdog

There is no breed of dog that cannot be trained. It does appear that some breeds are more difficult to get the desired response from than others. In many cases however, this has more to do with the trainer and his or her training methods than with the dog's inability to learn. With the proper approach, any dog that is not mentally deficient can be taught to be a good canine citizen. Many dog owners do not understand how a dog learns, nor do they realize they can be breed specific in their approach to training.

When teaching a Sheltie the things he must learn in order to be a good canine citizen, firm but fair is the philosophy that you should be guided by. The Shetland Sheepdog has a natural ability to learn, and handled properly the breed is a happy and determined worker.

Young Sheltie puppies have an amazing capacity to learn. This capacity is greater than most humans realize. It is important to remember though, these young puppies also forget with great speed unless they are reminded of what they have learned by continual reinforcement.

As Sheltie puppies leave the nest they begin their search for two things: a pack leader, and the rules set down by that leader

Your Sheltie must learn the rules of the household. Now that these two Tara Hill Sheltie pups are on the couch, they have to figure out how to get down!

by which they can abide. Too many owners fail miserably in supplying these very basic needs. Instead, the owner immediately begins to respond to the demands of the puppy and Sheltie puppies can quickly learn to be very demanding.

For example, a Sheltie puppy quickly learns he will be allowed into the house because he is whining, not because it can only enter the house when it is not whining. Instead of

Crate training is the quickest and easiest way to housebreak your Shetland Sheepdog.

learning the only way he will be fed is to follow a set procedure (i.e., sitting or lying down on command), the poorly educated Sheltie puppy learns leaping about the kitchen and creating a stir is what gets results.

The key to successful training lies in establishing the proper relationship between dog and owner. The owner or the owning family must be the pack leader and the individual or family must provide the rules by which the dog abides. Once this is established a Sheltie will live to be praised by his pack leader.

The Shetland Sheepdog is easily trained to do almost any task. It is important to remember, however, that the breed does not comprehend violent treatment nor does the Sheltie need it. Positive reinforcement is the key to successfully training a Sheltie. Always show your dog the right thing to do and be consistent in having him behave that way.

HOUSEBREAKING

The method of housebreaking we recommend is avoidance of accidents happening. We take a puppy outdoors to relieve himself after every meal, after every nap, and after every 15 or 20 minutes of playtime. We carry the puppy outdoors to avoid the opportunity of an accident occurring on the way.

Housebreaking your Sheltie becomes a much easier task with the use of a crate. Most breeders use the fiberglass type crates approved by the airlines for shipping live animals. They are easy to clean and can be used for the entire life of the dog.

Some first time dog owners may see the crate method of housebreaking as cruel. What they do not understand is that all dogs need a place of their own to retreat to. A puppy will soon look to his crate as his own private den.

Use of a crate reduces housetraining time down to an absolute minimum and avoids keeping a puppy under constant stress by incessantly correcting him for making mistakes in the house. The anti-crate advocates who consider it cruel to confine a puppy for any length of time do not seem to have a problem with constantly harassing and punishing the puppy because it has wet on the carpet and relieved himself behind the sofa.

Once your Sheltie is used to his crate he will come to think of it as a cozy den in which to retreat and relax.

Begin using the crate when you feed your Sheltie puppy. Keep the door closed and latched while the puppy is eating. When the meal is finished, open the crate and carry the puppy outdoors to the spot where you want him to learn to eliminate. In the event you do not have outdoor access, or will be away from home for long periods of time, begin housebreaking by placing newspapers in some out of the way corner that is easily accessible for the puppy. If you consistently take your puppy to the same spot you will reinforce the habit of going there for that purpose.

It is important that you do not let the puppy loose after eating. Young puppies will eliminate almost immediately after eating or drinking. They will also be ready to relieve themselves when they first wake up and after playing. If you keep a watchful eye on your puppy you will quickly learn when this is about to take place. A puppy usually circles and sniffs the floor just before he will relieve himself. Do not give your puppy an opportunity to learn that he can eliminate in the house! Your house training chores will be reduced considerably if you avoid bad habits beginning in the first place.

If you take your dog to the same place every time to eliminate, he will soon know what is expected of him. This Sheltie checks out the facilities at an interstate rest stop.

If you are not able to watch your puppy every minute, he should be in his crate with the door securely latched. Each time you put your puppy in his crate give him a small treat of some kind. Throw the treat to the back of the crate and encourage the puppy to walk in on his own. When he does so, praise the puppy and perhaps hand him another piece of the treat through the wires of the crate.

Do understand a Sheltie puppy of 8 to 12 weeks of age will not be able to contain himself for long periods of time. Puppies of that age must relieve themselves often, except at night. Your schedule must be adjusted accordingly. Also make sure your puppy has relieved himself at night before the last member of the family retires.

Your first priority in the morning is to get the puppy outdoors. Just how early this will take place will depend much more upon your puppy than upon you. If your Sheltie is like most others, there will be no doubt in your mind when he needs to be let out. You will also very quickly learn to tell the difference between the puppy's "emergency" signals and just unhappy grumbling. Do not test the young puppy's ability to contain himself. His vocal demand to be let out is confirmation that the housebreaking lesson is being learned.

Should you find it necessary to be away from home all day you will not be able to leave your puppy in a crate, but on the other hand, do not make the mistake of allowing him to roam the house or even a large room at will. Confine the puppy to a small room or partitioned-off area and cover the floor with newspaper. Make this area large enough so that the puppy will not have to relieve himself next to his bed, food, or water bowls. You will soon find the puppy will be inclined to use one particular spot to perform his bowel and bladder functions. When you are home you must take the puppy to this exact spot to eliminate at the appropriate time.

BASIC TRAINING

It is important for Shetland Sheepdog owners to remember that the breed thrives and grows on learning. The Sheltie has a great capacity to learn and if this ability is not activated in a positive manner by the dog's owner, the dog can and may become incredibly creative in ways that may well test patience beyond one's limits.

Another important factor to keep in mind when training a Sheltie is the breed's uncanny ability not only to think, but to think ahead. For this reason the Sheltie makes a top notch competitor in the obedience ring. There is a down side to this, however. Once a Sheltie learns a set procedure, it knows what is coming next and may just as easily go on to do this without another command. So, if you are training your Sheltie for formal obedience work do not train exactly the same thing each day. Vary the exercises and never do them in the order that they will be done in actual obedience competition.

Training should never take place when you are irritated, distressed, or preoccupied. Nor should you begin basic training in crowded or noisy places that will interfere with you or your dog's concentration. Once the commands are understood and learned you can begin testing your dog in public places, but at first the two of you should work in a place where you can concentrate fully upon each other.

Consistency is the key to training your Sheltie. Ch. Shekou's Candega Shalimar owned by Daphne Allen stands at attention.

The "No!" Command

There is no doubt whatsoever that one of the most important commands your Sheltie puppy will ever learn is the meaning of "no!" It is extremely important that your puppy learn this command just as soon as possible. One important piece of advice in using this and all other commands—never give a Sheltie a command you are not prepared and able to enforce! The only way a puppy learns to obey commands is to realize that once issued, commands must be complied with. Learning the "no" command should start the first day of the puppy's arrival at your home.

Leash Training

It is never too early to accustom your Sheltie puppy to his leash and collar. The leash and collar are your fail-safe ways of

Shetland Sheepdog puppies need to learn how to walk on a leash without pulling or tugging. keeping your dog under control. It may not be necessary for the puppy or adult Shetland Sheepdog to wear his collar and identification tags within the confines of your home, but no dog should ever leave home without a collar and without the leash held securely in your hand.

It is best to begin getting your puppy accustomed to his collar by leaving a soft collar around his neck for a few minutes at a time. Gradually extend the time you leave the collar on. Most Sheltie puppies become accustomed to their collar very quickly and after a few scratches to remove it, forget they are even wearing one.

While you are playing with the puppy, attach a lightweight leash to the collar. Do not try to guide the puppy at first. The point here is to accustom the puppy to the feeling of having something attached to the collar.

Encourage your puppy to follow you as you move away. Should the puppy be reluctant to cooperate, coax him along with a treat of some kind. Hold the treat in front of the puppy's nose to encourage him to follow you. Just as soon as the puppy takes a few steps toward you, praise him enthusiastically and continue to do so as you continue to move along.

Make the initial sessions short and fun. Continue the lessons in your home or yard until the puppy is completely unconcerned about the fact that he is on a leash. With a treat in one hand and the leash in the other you can begin to use both to guide the puppy in the direction you wish to go. Begin your first walks in front of the house and eventually extend them down the street and eventually around the block.

Even the youngest Shetland Sheepdog has a great capacity to learn. This baby is happily playing fetch with his owner.

The "Come" Command

The next most important lesson for the any puppy to learn is to come when called. Therefore is very important that the puppy learn his name as soon as possible. Constantly repeating the dog's name is what does the trick. Use the puppy's name every time you speak to him. "Want to go outside, Rex?" "Come Rex, come!"

Learning to "come" on command could save your Sheltie's life when the two of you venture out into the world. "Come" is the command a dog must understand has to be obeyed without question, but the dog should not associate that command with fear. Your dog's response to his name and the word "come" should always be associated with a pleasant experience such as great praise and petting or a food treat.

All too often novice trainers get very angry at their dog for not responding immediately to the "come" command. When the dog finally does come or after a chase, the owner scolds the dog for not obeying. The dog begins to associate "come" with an unpleasant result.

It is much easier to avoid the establishment of bad habits than it is to correct them once set. Avoid at all costs giving the "come" command unless you are sure your Sheltie puppy will come to you. The very young puppy is far more inclined to respond to learning the "come" command than the older dog who will be less dependent upon you.

Use the command initially when the puppy is already on his way to you, or give the command while walking or running away from the youngster. Clap your hands and sound very happy and excited about having the puppy join in on this "game."

Praise and play are the best way to encourage your Sheltie when training.

The very young Sheltie will normally want to stay as close to his owner as possible, especially in strange surroundings. When your puppy sees you moving away, his natural inclination will be to get close to you. This is a perfect time to use the "come" command.

Later, as a puppy grows more self confident and independent, you may want to attach a long leash or rope to the puppy's collar to ensure the correct response. Again, do not chase or punish your puppy for not obeying the "come" command. Doing so in the initial stages of training makes the youngster associate the command with something to fear and this will result in avoidance rather than the immediate positive response you desire. It is imperative that you praise your puppy and give him a treat when he does come to you, even if he voluntarily delays responding for many minutes.

The "Sit" and "Stay" Commands

Just as important to your Sheltie's safety (and your sanity!) as the "no!" command and learning to come when called are the "sit" and "stay" commands. Even very young puppies can learn the sit command quickly, especially if it appears to be a game and a food treat is involved.

Your puppy should always be on collar and leash for his lessons. Young puppies are not beyond getting up and walking away when they have decided you and your lessons are boring.

Give the "sit" command immediately before pushing down on your puppy's hindquarters or scooping his hind legs under him, molding him into a sit position. Praise the puppy lavishly when he does sit, even though it is you who made the action take place. Again, a food treat always seems to get the lesson across to the learning youngster.

Continue holding the dog's rear end down and repeat the "sit" command several times. If your dog makes an attempt to get up, repeat the command yet again while exerting pressure on the rear end until the correct position is assumed. Make your Sheltie stay in this position for increasing lengths of time.

Begin with a few seconds and increase the time as lessons progress over the following weeks.

Should your young student attempt to get up or to lie down he should be corrected by simply saying, "sit!" in a firm voice. This should be accompanied by returning the dog to the desired position. Only when you decide your dog should get up should he be allowed to do so.

Do not test a very young puppy's patience to the limits. Remember you are dealing with a baby. The attention span of any youngster, canine or human, is relatively short.

When you do decide your puppy can get up, call his name, say "OK" and make a big fuss over it. Praise and a food treat are in order every time your puppy responds correctly.

Once your puppy has mastered the "sit" lesson you may start on the "stay" command. With your dog on leash and facing you, command him to "sit," then take a step or two back. If your dog attempts to get up to follow firmly say, "Sit, stay!" While you are saying this raise your hand, palm toward the dog, and again command, "Stay!"

Any attempt on your dog's part to get up must be corrected at once, returning him to the sit position and repeating, "Stay!" Once your Sheltie begins to understand what you want, you can gradually increase the distance you step back. With a long leash attached to your dog's collar (even a clothesline will do), start with a few steps and gradually increase the distance to several yards. Your Sheltie will eventually learn the "sit, stay" command must be obeyed no matter how far away you are. Later on, with advanced training, your dog will learn the command is to be obeyed even when you move entirely out of sight.

As your Sheltie masters this lesson and is able to remain in the sit position for as long as you dictate, avoid calling the dog to you at first. This makes the dog overly anxious to get up and run to you. Instead, walk

The Nylabone® Frisbee™ is made with strength, scent, and originality and is great fun for you and your Sheltie.
The trademark Frisbee is used under license from Mattel Inc., California, USA.

Because of his intelligence and eagerness to please, the Sheltie can accomplish almost any task you ask of him. back to your dog and say "OK" which is a signal that the command is over. Later, when your Sheltie becomes more reliable in this respect, you can call him to you.

The "sit, stay" lesson can take considerable time and patience especially with the puppy whose attention span will be very short. It is best to keep the "stay" part of the lesson to a minimum until the puppy is at least five or six months old. Everything in a very young Sheltie's makeup urges him to stay close to you wherever you go. Forcing a very young puppy to operate against his natural instincts can be bewildering.

The "Down" Command

Once your Sheltie has mastered the "sit" and "stay" commands, you may begin work on "down." This is the single word command for lie down. Use the "down" command only when you want the dog to lie down. If you want your dog to get off your sofa or to stop jumping up on people use the "off" command. Do not interchange these two commands. Doing so will only serve to confuse your dog and evoking the right response will become next to impossible.

The "down" position is especially useful if you want your Sheltie to remain in a particular place for a long period of time. A dog is usually far more inclined to stay put when he is lying down than when he is sitting.

Teaching this command to your Sheltie may take more time and patience than the previous lessons. It is believed by some animal behaviorists that assuming the "down" position somehow represents submissiveness to the dog.

We recommend teaching the down from a standing position. Place one hand on the withers (top of the shoulders) and gently push down and back at the same time. This forces the dog to lower and fold back with the hind legs under him and the front legs out ahead. Give the down command as you apply the backward and downward pressure. This keeps the dog moving in one continuous movement, instead of sitting first and then lying down from the "sit" position. It also keeps the dog's decision making process directed toward one command. If the dog were to become distracted he might only remember to sit.

Also, if the dog is off lead and the "down" signal is given he will always assume the drop faster when he has learned the "one motion down." At the higher levels of obedience competition it is especially useful because the dog can go from the "stand" to the "down" position without ever moving a single foot.

The "Heel" Command

In learning to heel, your dog will walk on your left side with his shoulder next to your leg no matter which direction you

Teaching your Sheltie to heel will not only make daily walks more enjoyable, it will make him a better companion.

might go or how quickly you turn. Teaching your Shetland Sheepdog to heel will not only make your daily walks far more enjoyable, it will make him a far more tractable companion when the two of you are in crowded or confusing situations.

We have found a lightweight, link-chain training collar is very useful for the heeling lesson. It provides quick pressure around the neck and a snapping sound, both of which get the dog's attention. Erroneously referred to as a "choke collar," the link-chain collar used properly does not choke the dog. The pet shop at which you purchase the training collar will be able to show you the proper way to put this collar on your dog. Do not leave this collar on your puppy when training sessions are finished. Puppies are ingenious at getting their lower jaw or legs caught in the training chain. Changing to the link-chain collar at training time also signals your Sheltie that he must get down to the business at hand.

Proper training will assure that your dog will be welcomed in any situation. Your Sheltie will thank you for it!

When you begin training your puppy to walk along on the leash, you should accustom the youngster to walk on your left side. The leash should cross your body from the dog's collar to your right hand. The excess portion of the leash will be folded into your right hand, and your left hand on the leash will be used to make corrections with the leash.

A quick short jerk on the leash with your left hand will keep your dog from lunging side to side, pulling ahead or lagging back. As you make a correction give the "heel" command. Keep the leash slack as long as your dog maintains the proper position at your side.

If your dog begins to drift away, give the leash a sharp jerk and guide the dog back to the correct position and give the "heel" command. Do not pull on the lead with steady pressure. What is needed is a sharp but gentle jerking motion to get your dog's attention.

Training Classes

There are few limits to what a patient consistent Shetland Sheepdog owner can teach his or her dog. For advanced obedience work beyond the basics, it is wise for the Sheltie owner to consider local professional assistance. Professional trainers have had long standing experience in avoiding the pitfalls of obedience training and can help you to avoid these mistakes as well.

This training assistance can be obtained in many ways. Classes are particularly good for your Sheltie's socialization and attentiveness. The dog will learn that he must obey even when there are other dogs and people around that provide temptation to run off and play. There are free-of-charge classes at many parks and recreation facilities, as well as very formal and sometimes very expensive individual lessons with private trainers.

Shetland Sheepdogs are among the top performers in obedience and agility trials.

There are also some obedience schools that will take your Sheltie and train him for you. However, unless your schedule provides no time at all to train your own dog, having someone else train the dog for you would be last on our list of recommendations. The rapport that develops between the owner who has trained his or her Sheltie to be a pleasant companion and good canine citizen is very special—well worth the time and patience it requires to achieve.

VERSATILITY

The Sheltie's keen intelligence, energy, stamina, and desire to please has led to a variety of highly specialized roles. As a herding dog, Shetland Sheepdogs have been trained to formal trialing standards. Many Shelties are still used as all around farm dogs and will help fetch sheep, ducks, and cattle. Herding is just one of the myriad of activities the Shetland Sheepdog can be trained for.

Hearing and sight dogs: The Sheltie trained in this manner can be used in the home to help the hearing impaired by

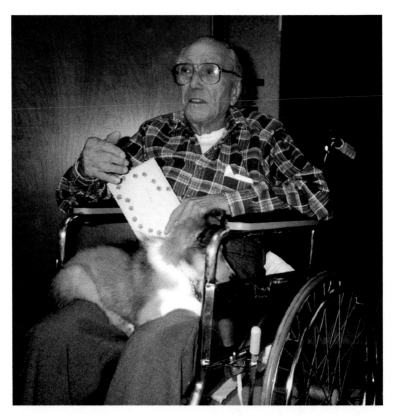

Shelties excel in the role of therapy dog. This young Sheltie brings a bit of sunshine to his friend at a convalescent home.

alerting the person that the door bell or telephone has rung. Sight assistance dogs can be trained to locate objects or help their restricted-vision owners to avoid falls.

Search and Rescue: Shelties can be used when there is need for a dog to go into a small space to see if a person is trapped under fallen debris or snow. Dogs that do so then sound the alarm for rescue teams.

Therapy dogs: Shetland Sheepdogs are widely used in children's hospitals as well as retirement and convalescent homes. Shelties love people and are extremely successful in providing residents and patients with the feeling that someone really cares about them. Many Shetland Sheepdog clubs throughout the country provide these services.

Obedience: Shelties make top obedience dogs. Their strong desire to please and willingness to work make them a fun dog to train. Most dog shows have a high percentage of Shelties entered in the obedience competitions. They are ringside favorites in that the dogs are such happy workers. Tails are always wagging and they are extremely eager to perform any task asked of them.

Agility: Shetland Sheepdogs are very agile. Most of the time Shelties will complete the agility courses at dog shows in record time without a flaw in their performance. Sometimes a Sheltie will be a real crowd pleaser with a great sense of humor. Once they have received a laugh from the crowd their performance only gets better.

Tracking and retrieving: This is an area that a Sheltie can do exceptionally well in, but do not ask a Sheltie to cross water. A Sheltie will do everything possible to avoid getting his feet wet and the breed generally does not like water. The Sheltie coat gets extremely heavy in water. The wet coat makes swimming very difficult.

Shetland Sheepdogs get a real thrill from participating in agility. Nikki owned by William Polliey shows his prowess at the weave poles.

With the proper training, there is nothing your versatile Sheltie can't do!

The positive side to this is that the breed can easily be taught to stay away from swimming pools. They not only prefer not to be near a pool, they will usually sound the alarm if an infant or toddler gets too close or falls into a pool.

There is actually no boundary to this unique breed's versatility. If the Shetland Sheepdog has any limitations at all they are usually due to human limitations. Above all, however, Shelties are ideal companions and friends. They have a love for their owners that is almost impossible to express in writing. If you have a problem and need an ear, your Sheltie will be first to sit at your side and listen. A Sheltie might not be able to solve your problem, but I guarantee you will feel better after you have shared what is bothering you.

To quote Elizabeth D. Whelen, the very well-known and highly respected breeder of the Pocono Shetland Sheepdogs, "There is no greater love, than the love of a Sheltie."

Only those who have experienced life with a Sheltie or who will do so in the future will be able to fully understand what Elizabeth Whelen meant.

SPORT of Purebred Dogs

by Judy Iby

Welcome to the exciting and sometimes frustrating sport of dogs. No doubt you are trying to learn more about dogs or you wouldn't be deep into this book. This section covers the basics that may entice you, further your knowledge and help you to understand the dog world.

Dog showing has been a very popular sport for a long time and has been taken quite seriously by some. Others only enjoy it as a hobby.

Successful showing requires dedication and preparation, but most of all, it should be an enjoyable experience for dogs and owners alike.

The Kennel Club in England was formed in 1859, the American Kennel Club was established in 1884 and the Canadian Kennel Club was formed in 1888. The purpose of these clubs was to register purebred dogs and maintain their Stud Books. In the beginning, the concept of registering dogs was not readily accepted. More than 36 million dogs have been enrolled in the AKC Stud Book since its inception in 1888. Presently the kennel clubs not only register dogs but adopt and enforce rules and regulations governing dog shows, obedience trials and field trials. Over the years they have fostered and encouraged interest in the health and welfare of the purebred dog. They routinely donate funds to veterinary research for study on genetic disorders.

Below are the addresses of the kennel clubs in the United States, Great Britain and Canada.

The American Kennel Club
51 Madison Avenue
New York, NY 10010
(Their registry is located at: 5580 Centerview Drive, STE 200, Raleigh, NC 27606-3390)

The Kennel Club
1 Clarges Street
Piccadilly, London, W1Y 8AB, England

The Canadian Kennel Club
111 Eglinton Avenue
East Toronto, Ontario M6S 4V7
Canada

Today there are numerous activities that are enjoyable for both the dog and the handler. Some of the activities include conformation showing, obedience competition, tracking, agility, the Canine Good Citizen Certificate, and a wide range of instinct tests that vary from breed to breed. Where you start depends upon your goals which early on may not be readily apparent.

Candega's Panache's obvious beauty and grace have earned him both his American and Canadian championships.

Puppy Kindergarten

Every puppy will benefit from this class. PKT is the foundation for all future dog activities from conformation to "couch potatoes." Pet owners should make an effort to attend even if they never expect to show their dog. The class is designed for puppies about three months of age with graduation at approximately five months of age. All the puppies will be in the same age group and, even though some may be a little unruly, there should not be any real problem. This class will teach the puppy some beginning obedience. As in all obedience classes the owner learns how to train his own dog. The PKT class gives the puppy the opportunity to interact with other puppies in the same age group and exposes him to strangers, which is very important. Some dogs grow up with behavior problems, one of them being fear of strangers. As you can see, there can be much to gain from this class.

Every Shetland Sheepdog can benefit from basic obedience training.

There are some basic obedience exercises that every dog should learn. Some of these can be started with puppy kindergarten.

Conformation

Conformation showing is our oldest dog show sport. This type of showing is based on the dog's appearance—that is his structure, movement and attitude. When considering this type of showing, you need to be aware of your breed's standard and be able to evaluate your dog compared to that standard. The breeder of your puppy or other experienced breeders would be good sources for such an evaluation. Puppies can go through lots of changes over a period of time. Many puppies start out as promising hopefuls and then after maturing may be disappointing as show candidates. Even so this should not deter them from being excellent pets.

Usually conformation training classes are offered by the local kennel or obedience clubs. These are excellent places for training puppies. The puppy should be able to walk on a lead before entering such a class. Proper ring procedure and technique for posing (stacking) the dog will be demonstrated as well as gaiting the dog. Usually certain patterns are used in the ring such as the triangle or the "L." Conformation class, like the PKT class, will give your youngster the opportunity to socialize with different breeds of dogs and humans too.

It takes some time to learn the routine of conformation showing. Usually one starts at the puppy matches that may be AKC Sanctioned or Fun Matches. These matches are generally for puppies from two or three months to a year old, and there may be classes for the adult over the age of 12 months. Similar to point shows, the classes are divided by sex and after completion of the classes in that breed or variety, the class winners compete for Best of Breed or Variety. The winner goes on to compete in the Group and the Group winners compete for Best in Match. No championship points are awarded for match wins.

A few matches can be great training for puppies even though there is no intention to go on showing. Matches enable the puppy to meet new people and be handled by a stranger— the judge. It is also a change of environment, which broadens the horizon for both dog and handler. Matches and other dog activities boost the confidence of the handler and especially the younger handlers.

Earning an AKC championship is built on a point system, which is different from Great Britain. To become an AKC Champion of Record the dog must earn 15 points. The number of points earned each time depends upon the number of dogs in competition. The number of points available at each show depends upon the breed, its sex and the location of the show. The United States is divided into ten AKC zones. Each zone has its own set of points. The purpose of the zones is to try to equalize the points available from breed to breed and area to area.The AKC adjusts the point scale annually.

The number of points that can be won at a show are between one and five. Three-, four- and five-point wins are considered majors. Not only does the dog need 15 points won under three different judges, but those points must include two majors under two different judges. Canada also works on a point system but majors are not required.

Dogs always show before bitches. The classes available to those seeking points are: Puppy (which may be divided into 6 to 9 months and 9 to 12 months); 12 to 18 months; Novice; Bred-by-Exhibitor; American-bred; and Open. The class winners of the same sex of each breed or variety compete against each other for Winners Dog and Winners Bitch. A Reserve Winners Dog and Reserve Winners Bitch are also awarded but do not carry any points unless the Winners win is disallowed by AKC. The Winners Dog and Bitch compete with the specials (those dogs that have attained championship) for Best of Breed or Variety, Best of Winners and Best of Opposite Sex. It is possible to pick up an extra point or even a major if the points are higher for the defeated winner than those of Best of Winners. The latter would get the higher total from the defeated winner.

In conformation, your Sheltie will be evaluated on how closely he conforms to the standard of the breed

At an all-breed show, each Best of Breed or Variety winner will go on to his respective Group and then the Group winners will compete against each other for Best in Show. There are seven Groups: Sporting, Hounds, Working, Terriers, Toys, Non-Sporting and Herding. Obviously there are no Groups at speciality shows (those shows that have only one breed or a show such as the American Spaniel Club's Flushing Spaniel Show, which is for all flushing spaniel breeds).

Earning a championship in England is somewhat different since they do not have a point system. Challenge Certificates are awarded if the judge feels the dog is deserving regardless of the number of dogs in competition. A dog must earn three Challenge Certificates under three different judges, with at least one of these Certificates being won after the age of 12 months. Competition is very strong and entries may be higher than they are in the U.S. The Kennel Club's Challenge Certificates are only available at Championship Shows.

In England, The Kennel Club regulations require that certain dogs, Border Collies and Gundog breeds, qualify in a working capacity (i.e., obedience or field trials) before becoming a full Champion. If they do not qualify in the working aspect, then they are designated a Show Champion, which is equivalent to the AKC's Champion of Record. A Gundog may be granted the title of Field Trial Champion (FT Ch.) if it passes all the tests in the field but would also have to qualify in conformation before becoming a full Champion. A Border Collie that earns the title of Obedience Champion (Ob Ch.) must also qualify in the conformation ring before becoming a Champion.

The U.S. doesn't have a designation full Champion but does award for Dual and Triple Champions. The Dual Champion must be a Champion of Record, and either Champion Tracker, Herding Champion, Obedience Trial Champion or Field Champion. Any dog that has been awarded the titles of Champion of Record, and any two of the following: Champion Tracker, Herding Champion, Obedience Trial Champion or Field Champion, may be designated as a Triple Champion.

The shows in England seem to put more emphasis on breeder judges than those in the U.S. There is much competition within the breeds. Therefore the quality of the individual breeds should be very good. In the United States we tend to have more "all around judges" (those that judge multiple breeds) and use the breeder judges at the specialty shows. Breeder judges are more familiar with their own breed since they are actively breeding that breed or did so at one time. Americans emphasize Group and Best in Show wins and promote them accordingly.

The shows in England can be very large and extend over several days, with the Groups being scheduled on different days. Though multi-day shows are not common in the U.S., there are cluster shows, where several different clubs will use the same show site over consecutive days.

Westminster Kennel Club is our most prestigious show although the entry is limited to 2500. In recent years, entry has been limited to Champions. This show is more formal than the majority of the shows with the judges wearing formal attire and the handlers fashionably dressed. In most instances the quality of the dogs is superb. After all, it is a show of Champions. It is a good show to study the AKC registered breeds and is by far the most exciting—especially since it is televised! WKC is one of the few shows in this country that is still benched. This means the dog must be in his benched area during the show hours except when he is being groomed, in the ring, or being exercised.

Typically, the handlers are very particular about their appearances. They are careful not to wear something that will detract from their dog but will perhaps enhance it. American ring procedure is quite formal compared to that of other countries. There is a certain etiquette expected between the judge and exhibitor and among the other exhibitors. Of course it is not always the case but the judge is supposed to be polite, not engaging in small talk or acknowledging how well he knows the handler. There is a more informal and relaxed atmosphere at the shows in other countries. For instance, the dress code is more casual. I can see where this might be more fun for the exhibitor and especially for the novice. The U.S. is very handler-oriented in many of the

To the victor goes the spoils! Laddie and his owner Trevor Parkin show off the rewards of hard work and dedication.

breeds. It is true, in most instances, that the experienced professional handler can present the dog better and will have a feel for what a judge likes.

In England, Crufts is The Kennel Club's own show and is most assuredly the largest dog show in the world. They've been known to have an entry of nearly 20,000, and the show lasts four days. Entry is only gained by qualifying through winning in specified classes at another Championship Show. Westminster is strictly conformation, but Crufts exhibitors and spectators enjoy not only conformation but obedience, agility and a multitude of exhibitions as well. Obedience was admitted in 1957 and agility in 1983.

Ch. Tara Hill California Poppy bred by Linda and Rick Churchill is a shining example of a Shetland Sheepdog.

If you are handling your own dog, please give some consideration to your apparel. For sure the dress code at matches is more informal than the point shows. However, you should wear something a little more appropriate than beach attire or ragged jeans and bare feet. If you check out the handlers and see what is presently fashionable, you'll catch on. Men usually dress with a shirt and tie and a nice sports coat. Whether you are male or female, you will want to wear comfortable clothes and shoes. You need to be able to run with your dog and you certainly don't want to take a chance of falling and hurting yourself. Heaven forbid, if nothing else, you'll upset your dog. Women usually wear a dress or two-piece outfit, preferably with pockets to carry bait, comb, brush, etc. In this case men are the lucky ones with all their pockets. Ladies, think about where your dress will be if you need to kneel on the floor and also think about running. Does it allow freedom to do so?

You need to take along dog; crate; ex pen (if you use

Well-trained dogs that have been properly socialized enjoy each other's company. This Sheltie and Shih Tzu are roommates and friends.

Junior showmanship is a great way to build self confidence for both the child and the dog. Kelly Churchill and Ch. Sandalwood's O'Scotia compete at the Santiago SSC Specialty.

one); extra newspaper; water pail and water; all required grooming equipment, including hair dryer and extension cord; table; chair for you; bait for dog and lunch for you and friends; and, last but not least, clean up materials, such as plastic bags, paper towels, and perhaps a bath towel and some shampoo—just in case. Don't forget your entry confirmation and directions to the show.

If you are showing in obedience, then you will want to wear pants. Many of our top obedience handlers wear pants that are color-coordinated with their dogs. The philosophy is that imperfections in the black dog will be less obvious next to your black pants.

Whether you are showing in conformation, Junior Showmanship or obedience, you need to watch the clock and be sure you are not late. It is customary to pick up your conformation armband a few minutes before the start of the class. They will not wait for you and if you are on the show grounds and not in the ring, you will upset everyone. It's a little more complicated picking up your obedience armband if you show later in the class. If you have not picked up your armband and they get to your number, you may not be allowed to show. It's best to pick up your armband early, but then you may show earlier than expected if other handlers don't pick up. Customarily all conflicts should be discussed with the judge prior to the start of the class.

To become a Canine Good Citizen, your Sheltie must be able to get along with all kinds of people. Stryker and Rocket have certainly passed the test!

Junior Showmanship

The Junior Showmanship Class is a wonderful way to build self confidence even if there are no aspirations of staying with the dog-show game later in life. Frequently, Junior Showmanship becomes the background of those who become successful exhibitors/handlers in the future. In some instances it is taken very seriously, and success is measured in terms of wins. The Junior Handler is judged solely on his ability and skill in presenting his dog. The dog's conformation is not to be considered by the judge. Even so the condition and grooming of the dog may be a reflection upon the handler.

Usually the matches and point shows include different classes. The Junior Handler's dog may be entered in a breed or obedience class and even shown by another person in that class. Junior Showmanship classes are usually divided by age and perhaps sex. The age is determined by the handler's age on the day of the show.

Canine Good Citizen

The AKC sponsors a program to encourage dog owners to train their dogs. Local clubs perform the pass/fail tests, and

103

dogs who pass are awarded a Canine Good Citizen Certificate. Proof of vaccination is required at the time of participation. The test includes:

1. Accepting a friendly stranger.
2. Sitting politely for petting.
3. Appearance and grooming.
4. Walking on a loose leash.
5. Walking through a crowd.
6. Sit and down on command/staying in place.
7. Come when called.
8. Reaction to another dog.
9. Reactions to distractions.
10. Supervised separation.

If more effort was made by pet owners to accomplish these exercises, fewer dogs would be cast off to the humane shelter.

OBEDIENCE

Obedience is necessary, without a doubt, but it can also become a wonderful hobby or even an obsession. Obedience classes and competition can provide wonderful companionship, not only with your dog but with your classmates or fellow competitors. It is always gratifying to discuss your dog's problems with others who have had similar experiences. The AKC acknowledged Obedience around 1936, and it has changed tremendously even though many of the exercises are basically the same. Today, obedience competition is just that—very competitive. Even so, it is possible for every obedience exhibitor to come home a winner (by earning qualifying scores) even though he/she may not earn a placement in the class.

Most of the obedience titles are awarded after earning three qualifying scores (legs) in the appropriate class under three different judges. These classes offer a perfect score of 200, which is extremely rare. Each of the class exercises has its own point value. A leg is earned after receiving a score of at least 170 and at least 50 percent of the points available in each exercise. The titles are:

Companion Dog—CD

Companion Dog Excellent—CDX

Utility Dog—UD

After achieving the UD title, you may feel inclined to go after the UDX and/or OTCh. The UDX (Utility Dog Excellent) title went into effect in January 1994. It is not easily attained. The title requires qualifying simultaneously ten times in Open B and Utility B but not necessarily at consecutive shows.

The OTCh (Obedience Trial Champion) is awarded after the dog has earned his UD and then goes on to earn 100 championship points, a first place in Utility, a first place in Open and another first place in either class. The placements must be won under three different judges at all-breed obedience trials. The points are determined by the number of dogs competing in the Open B and Utility B classes. The OTCh title precedes the dog's name.

Obedience matches (AKC Sanctioned, Fun, and Show and Go) are usually available. Usually *This Shetland Sheepdog* they are sponsored by the local *performs drop on* obedience clubs. When preparing *recall in the open* an obedience dog for a title, you *obedience class.* will find matches very helpful. Fun

Matches and Show and Go Matches are more lenient in allowing you to make corrections in the ring. This type of training is usually very necessary for the Open and Utility Classes. AKC Sanctioned Obedience Matches do not allow corrections in the ring since they must abide by the AKC Obedience Regulations. If you are interested in showing in obedience, then you should contact the AKC for a copy of the Obedience Regulations.

TRACKING

Tracking is officially classified obedience. There are three tracking titles available: Tracking Dog (TD), Tracking Dog Excellent (TDX), Variable Surface Tracking (VST). If all three tracking titles are obtained, then the dog officially becomes a CT (Champion Tracker). The CT will go in front of the dog's name.

A TD may be earned anytime and does not have to follow the other obedience titles. There are many exhibitors that prefer tracking to obedience, and there are others who do both.

AGILITY

Agility was first introduced by John Varley in England at the Crufts Dog Show, February 1978, but Peter Meanwell, competitor and judge, actually developed the idea. It was officially recognized in the early '80s. Agility is extremely popular in England and Canada and growing in popularity in the U.S. The AKC acknowledged agility in August 1994. Dogs must be at least 12 months of age to be entered. It is a fascinating sport that the dog, handler and spectators enjoy to

The Sheltie's nimbleness is a reminder of the days when he worked the rugged terrain of his native Shetland Islands.

the utmost. Agility is a spectator sport! The dog performs off lead. The handler either runs with his dog or positions himself on the course and directs his dog with verbal and hand signals over a timed course over or through a variety of obstacles including a time out or pause. One of the main drawbacks to agility is finding a place to train. The obstacles take up a lot of space and it is very time consuming to put up and take down courses.

Tracking allows your Sheltie to do what dogs do best— use his nose. This Sheltie searches for articles in a scent discrimination test.

The titles earned at AKC agility trials are Novice Agility Dog (NAD), Open Agility Dog (OAD), Agility Dog Excellent (ADX), and

The Shetland Sheepdog is always a ringside favorite as his joy at competing in obedience and agility is evident in his expression.

Master Agility Excellent (MAX). In order to acquire an agility title, a dog must earn a qualifying score in its respective class on three separate occasions under two different judges. The MAX will be

awarded after earning ten qualifying scores in the Agility Excellent Class.

PERFORMANCE TESTS

During the last decade the American Kennel Club has promoted performance tests–those events that test the different breeds' natural abilities. This type of event encourages a handler to devote even more time to his dog and retain the natural instincts of his breed heritage. It is an important part of the wonderful world of dogs.

Herding Titles

For all Herding breeds and Rottweilers and Samoyeds.

Entrants must be at least nine months of age and dogs with limited registration (ILP) are eligible. The Herding program is divided into Testing and Trial sections. The goal is to demonstrate proficiency in herding livestock in diverse situations. The titles offered are Herding Started (HS), Herding Intermediate (HI), and Herding Excellent (HX). Upon completion of the HX a Herding Championship may be earned after accumulating 15 championship points.

The above information has been taken from the AKC Guidelines for the appropriate events.

GENERAL INFORMATION

Obedience, tracking and agility allow the purebred dog with an Indefinite Listing Privilege (ILP) number or a limited registration to be exhibited and earn titles. Application must be made to the AKC for an ILP number.

The American Kennel Club publishes a monthly *Events* magazine that is part of the *Gazette*, their official journal for the sport of purebred dogs. The *Events* section lists upcoming shows and the secretary or superintendent for them. The majority of the conformation shows in the U.S. are overseen by licensed superintendents. Generally the entry closing date is approximately two-and-a-half weeks before the actual show. Point shows are fairly expensive, while the match shows cost about one third of the point show entry fee. Match shows usually take entries the day of the show but some are pre-entry. The best way to find match show information is through your local kennel club. Upon asking, the AKC can provide you with a list of superintendents, and you can write and ask to be put on their mailing lists.

Obedience trial and tracking test information is available through the AKC. Frequently these events are not superintended, but put on by the host club. Therefore you would make the entry with the event's secretary.

As you have read, there are numerous activities you can share with your dog. Regardless what you do, it does take teamwork. Your dog can only benefit from your attention and training. We hope this chapter has enlightened you and hope, if nothing else, you will attend a show here and there. Perhaps you will start with a puppy kindergarten class, and who knows where it may lead!

Herding trials allow your Sheltie to demonstrate his inherent talents and natural abilities. Peggy Duezabou trains with her Sheltie for a herding test.

HEALTH CARE   by Judy Iby

Veterinary medicine has become far more sophisticated than what was available to our ancestors. This can be attributed to the increase in household pets and consequently the demand for better care for them. Also human medicine has become far more complex. Today diagnostic testing in veterinary medicine parallels human diagnostics. Because of better technology we can expect our pets to live healthier lives thereby increasing their life spans.

THE FIRST CHECK UP

You will want to take your new puppy/dog in for its first check up within 48 to 72 hours after acquiring it. Many breeders strongly recommend this check up and so do the humane shelters. A puppy/dog can appear healthy but it may have a serious problem that is not apparent to the layman.

Maternal antibodies protect puppies from disease the first few weeks of life. Vaccinations are needed because the antibodies are only temporarily effective.

Most pets have some type of a minor flaw that may never cause a real problem.

Unfortunately if he/she should have a serious problem, you will want to consider the consequences of keeping the pet and the attachments that will be formed, which may be broken prematurely.

Keep in mind there are many healthy dogs looking for good homes.

This first check up is a good time to establish yourself with the veterinarian and learn the office policy regarding their hours and how they handle emergencies. Usually the breeder or another conscientious pet owner is a good reference for locating a capable veterinarian. You should be aware that not all veterinarians give the same quality of service. Please do not make your selection on the least expensive clinic, as they may be short changing your pet. There is the possibility that eventually it will cost you more due to improper diagnosis, treatment, etc. If you are selecting a new veterinarian, feel free to ask for a tour of the clinic. You should inquire about making an appointment for a tour since all clinics are working clinics, and therefore may not be available all day for sightseers. You may worry less if you see where your pet will be spending the day if he ever needs to be hospitalized.

Your veterinarian will put your Sheltie pup on a immunization schedule to protect him from disease.

The Physical Exam

Your veterinarian will check your pet's overall condition, which includes listening to the heart; checking the respiration; feeling the abdomen, muscles and joints; checking the mouth, which includes the gum color and signs of gum disease along with plaque buildup; checking the ears for signs of an infection or ear mites; examining the eyes; and, last but not least, checking the condition of the skin and coat.

He should ask you questions regarding your pet's eating and elimination habits and invite you to relay your questions. It is a good idea to prepare a list so as not to forget anything. He should discuss the proper diet and the quantity to be fed. If this should differ from your breeder's recommendation, then you should convey to him the breeder's choice and see if he approves. If he recommends changing the diet, then this should be done over a few days so as not to cause a gastrointestinal upset. It is customary to take in a fresh stool sample (just a small amount) for a test for intestinal parasites. It must be fresh, preferably within 12 hours, since the eggs hatch quickly and after hatching will not be observed under the microscope. If your pet isn't obliging then, usually the technician can take one in the clinic.

A puppy should be taken to the veterinarian within the first 48 hours after you acquire him.

IMMUNIZATIONS

It is important that you take your puppy/dog's vaccination record with you on your first visit. In case of a puppy, presumably the breeder has seen to the vaccinations up to the time you acquired custody. Veterinarians differ in their vaccination protocol. It is not unusual for your puppy to have received vaccinations for distemper, hepatitis, leptospirosis, parvovirus and parainfluenza every two to three weeks from the age of five or six weeks. Usually this is a combined injection and is typically called the DHLPP. The DHLPP is given through at least 12 to 14 weeks of age, and it is customary to continue with another parvovirus vaccine at 16 to 18 weeks. You may wonder why so many immunizations are necessary. No one knows for sure when the puppy's maternal antibodies are gone, although it is customarily accepted that distemper antibodies are gone by 12 weeks. Usually parvovirus antibodies are gone by 16 to 18 weeks of age. However, it is possible for the maternal antibodies to be gone at a much earlier age or even a later age. Therefore immunizations are started at an early age. The vaccine will not give immunity as long as there are maternal antibodies.

The rabies vaccination is given at three or six months of age depending on your local laws. A vaccine for bordetella (kennel cough) is advisable and can be given anytime from the age of five weeks. The coronavirus is not commonly given unless there is a problem locally. The Lyme vaccine is necessary in endemic areas. Lyme disease has been reported in 47 states.

Distemper

This is virtually an incurable disease. If the dog recovers, he is subject to severe nervous disorders. The virus attacks every

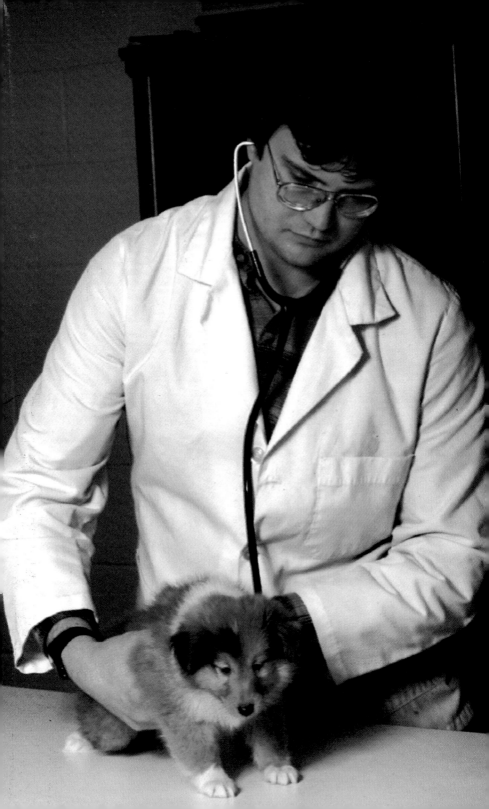

tissue in the body and resembles a bad cold with a fever. It can cause a runny nose and eyes and cause gastrointestinal disorders, including a poor appetite, vomiting and diarrhea. The virus is carried by raccoons, foxes, wolves, mink and other dogs. Unvaccinated youngsters and senior citizens are very susceptible. This is still a common disease.

Hepatitis

This is a virus that is most serious in very young dogs. It is spread by contact with an infected animal or its stool or urine. The virus affects the liver and kidneys and is characterized by high fever, depression and lack of appetite. Recovered animals may be afflicted with chronic illnesses.

Your Shetland Sheepdog will need regular check-ups to maintain his good health and prevent potential problems.

Leptospirosis

This is a bacterial disease transmitted by contact with the urine of an infected dog, rat or other wildlife. It produces

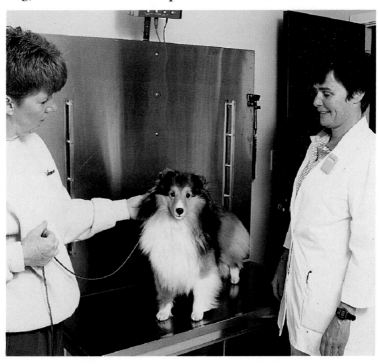

Your Sheltie can be subject to fleas and ticks when outside. Check your dog's coat thoroughly for any parasites after playing outdoors.

severe symptoms of fever, depression, jaundice and internal bleeding and was fatal before the vaccine was developed. Recovered dogs can be carriers, and the disease can be transmitted from dogs to humans.

Parvovirus

This was first noted in the late 1970s and is still a fatal disease. However, with proper vaccinations, early diagnosis and prompt treatment, it is a manageable disease. It attacks the bone marrow and intestinal tract. The symptoms include depression, loss of appetite, vomiting, diarrhea and collapse. Immediate medical attention is of the essence.

Rabies

This is shed in the saliva and is carried by raccoons, skunks, foxes, other dogs and cats. It attacks nerve tissue, resulting in paralysis and death. Rabies can be transmitted to people and is virtually always fatal. This disease is reappearing in the suburbs.

Bordetella (Kennel Cough)

The symptoms are coughing, sneezing, hacking and retching accompanied by nasal discharge usually lasting from a few days to several weeks. There are several disease-producing organisms responsible for this disease. The present vaccines are helpful but do not protect for all the strains. It usually is not life threatening but in some instances it can progress to a serious bronchopneumonia. The disease is highly contagious. The vaccination should be given routinely for dogs that come in contact with other dogs, such as through boarding, training class or visits to the groomer.

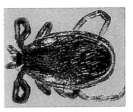

The deet tick is the most common carrier of Lyme disease. Photo courtesy of Virbac Laboratories, Inc., Fort Worth, Texas.

Coronavirus

This is usually self limiting and not life threatening. It was first noted in the late '70s about a year before parvovirus. The virus produces a yellow/brown stool and there may be depression, vomiting and diarrhea.

Lyme Disease

This was first diagnosed in the United States in 1976 in Lyme, CT in people who lived in close proximity to the deer tick. Symptoms may include acute lameness, fever, swelling of joints and loss of appetite. Your veterinarian can advise you if you live in an endemic area.

After your puppy has completed his puppy vaccinations, you will continue to booster the DHLPP once a year. It is customary to booster the rabies one year after the first vaccine and then, depending on where you live, it should be boostered every year or every three years. This depends on your local laws. The Lyme and corona vaccines are boostered annually and it is recommended that the bordetella be boostered every six to eight months.

A young puppy should be healthy looking and curious about the world around him. Ten-week-old Tara Hill Blueberry Buttons owned by Bonnie Smith.

ANNUAL VISIT

I would like to impress the importance of the annual check up, which would include the booster vaccinations, check for intestinal parasites and test for heartworm. Today in our very busy world it is rush, rush and see "how much you can get for how little." Unbelievably, some non-veterinary businesses have entered into the vaccination business. More harm than good can come to your dog through improper vaccinations, possibly from inferior vaccines and/or the wrong schedule. More than likely you truly care about your companion dog and over the years you have devoted much time and expense to his well being. Perhaps you are unaware that a vaccination is not just a vaccination. There is more involved. Please, please follow through with regular physical examinations. It is so important for your veterinarian to know your dog and this is especially true during middle age through the geriatric years. More than likely your older dog will require more than one physical a year. The annual physical is good preventive medicine. Through early diagnosis and subsequent treatment your dog can maintain a longer and better quality of life.

INTESTINAL PARASITES

Hookworms

These are almost microscopic intestinal worms that can cause anemia and therefore serious problems, including death, in young puppies. Hookworms can be transmitted to humans through penetration of the skin. Puppies may be born with them.

Roundworms

These are spaghetti-like worms that can cause a potbellied appearance and dull coat along with more severe symptoms,

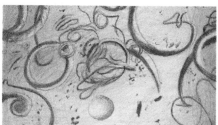

Whipworms are hard to find without a microscope and this is best left for the veterinarian. Pictured here are adult whipworms.

such as vomiting, diarrhea and coughing. Puppies acquire these while in the mother's uterus and through lactation. Both hookworms and roundworms may be acquired through ingestion.

Roundworm eggs, as would be seen on a fecal evaluation. The eggs must develop for at least 12 days before they are infective.

Whipworms

These have a three-month life cycle and are not acquired through the dam. They cause intermittent diarrhea usually with mucus. Whipworms are possibly the most difficult worm to eradicate. Their eggs are very resistant to most environmental factors and can last for years until the proper conditions enable them to mature. Whipworms are seldom seen in the stool.

Intestinal parasites are more prevalent in some areas than others. Climate, soil and contamination are big factors contributing to the incidence of intestinal parasites. Eggs are passed in the stool, lay on the ground and then become infective in a certain number of days. Each of the above worms has a different life cycle. Your best chance of becoming and remaining worm-free is to always pooper-scoop your yard. A fenced-in yard keeps stray dogs out, which is certainly helpful.

I would recommend having a fecal examination on your dog twice a year or more often if there is a problem. If your dog has a positive fecal sample, then he will be given the appropriate medication and you will be asked to bring back another stool sample in a certain period of time (depending on the type of worm) and then be rewormed. This process goes on until he has at least two negative samples. The different types of worms require different medications. You will be wasting your money and doing your dog an injustice by buying over-the-counter medication without first consulting your veterinarian.

OTHER INTERNAL PARASITES

Coccidiosis and Giardiasis

These protozoal infections usually affect puppies, especially

119

in places where large numbers of puppies are brought together. Older dogs may harbor these infections but do not show signs unless they are stressed. Symptoms include diarrhea, weight loss and lack of appetite. These infections are not always apparent in the fecal examination.

Tapeworms

Seldom apparent on fecal floatation, they are diagnosed frequently as rice-like segments around the dog's anus and the base of the tail. Tapeworms are long, flat and ribbon like, sometimes several feet in length, and made up of many segments about five-eighths of an inch long. The two most common types of tapeworms found in the dog are:

(1) First the larval form of the flea tapeworm parasite must mature in an intermediate host, the flea, before it can become infective. Your dog acquires this by ingesting the flea through licking and chewing.

(2) Rabbits, rodents and certain large game animals serve as intermediate hosts for other species of tapeworms. If your dog should eat one of these infected hosts, then he can acquire tapeworms.

Heartworm Disease

This is a worm that resides in the heart and adjacent blood vessels of the lung that produces microfilaria, which circulate in the bloodstream. It is possible for a dog to be infected with any number of worms from one to a hundred that can be 6 to 14 inches long. It is a life-threatening disease, expensive to treat and easily prevented. Depending on where you live, your veterinarian may recommend a preventive year-round and either an annual or semiannual blood test. The most common preventive is given once a month.

External Parasites

Fleas

These pests are not only the dog's worst enemy but also enemy to the owner's pocketbook. Preventing is less expensive than treating, but regardless we'd prefer to spend our money elsewhere. Likely, the majority of our dogs are allergic to the bite of a flea, and in many cases it only takes one flea bite. The protein in the flea's saliva is the culprit. Allergic dogs have a reaction, which usually results in a "hot spot." More than likely such a reaction will involve a trip to the veterinarian for treatment. Yes, prevention is less expensive. Fortunately today there are several good products available.

If there is a flea infestation, no one product is going to correct the problem. Not only will the dog require treatment so will the environment. In general flea collars are not very effective although there is now available an "egg" collar that will kill the eggs on the dog. Dips are the most economical but they are messy. There are some effective shampoos and treatments available through pet shops and veterinarians. An oral tablet arrived on the American market in 1995 and was popular in Europe the previous year. It sterilizes the female flea but will not kill adult fleas.

Your Sheltie's ears should be checked regularly and kept clean and free of waxy build-up.

Therefore the tablet, which is given monthly, will decrease the flea population but is not a "cure-all." Those dogs that suffer from flea-bite allergy will still be subjected to the bite of the flea. Another popular parasiticide is permethrin, which is applied to the back of the dog in one or two places depending on the dog's weight. This product works as a repellent causing the flea to get "hot feet" and jump off. Do not confuse this product with some of the organophosphates that are also applied to the dog's back.

Some products are not usable on young puppies. Treating fleas should be done under your veterinarian's guidance. Frequently it is necessary to combine products and the layman does not have the knowledge regarding possible toxicities. It is hard to believe but there are a few dogs that do have a natural resistance to fleas. Nevertheless it would be wise to treat all pets at the same time. Don't forget your cats. Cats just love to prowl the neighborhood and consequently return with unwanted guests.

Adult fleas live on the dog but their eggs drop off the dog into the environment. There they go through four larval stages before reaching adulthood, and thereby are able to jump back on the poor unsuspecting dog. The cycle resumes and takes between 21 to 28 days under ideal conditions. There are environmental products available that will kill both the adult fleas and the larvae.

Ticks

Ticks carry Rocky Mountain Spotted Fever, Lyme disease and can cause tick paralysis. They should be removed with tweezers, trying to pull out the head. The jaws carry disease. There is a tick preventive collar that does an excellent job. The ticks automatically back out on those dogs wearing collars.

Sarcoptic Mange

This is a mite that is difficult to find on skin scrapings. The pinnal reflex is a good indicator of this disease. Rub the ends of the pinna (ear) together and the dog will start scratching with his foot. Sarcoptes are highly contagious to other dogs and to humans although they do not live long on humans. They cause intense itching.

Demodectic Mange

This is a mite that is passed from the dam to her puppies. It affects youngsters age three to ten months. Diagnosis is confirmed by skin scraping. Small areas of alopecia around the eyes, lips and/or forelegs become visible. There is little itching

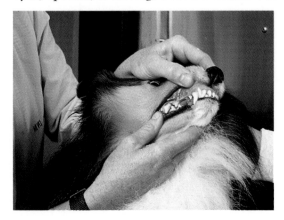

An thorough oral examination should be a part of your Shetland Sheepdog's annual check-up.

unless there is a secondary bacterial infection. Some breeds are afflicted more than others.

Cheyletiella
This causes intense itching and is diagnosed by skin scraping. It lives in the outer layers of the skin of dogs, cats, rabbits and humans. Yellow-gray scales may be found on the back and the rump, top of the head and the nose.

Toys, like Nylabones®, will help keep your Shetland Sheepdog's teeth clean while keeping him busy and out of mischief.

To Breed or Not To Breed
More than likely your breeder has requested that you have your puppy neutered or spayed. Your breeder's request is based on what is healthiest for your dog and what is most beneficial for your breed. Experienced and conscientious breeders devote many years into

Your Sheltie puppy is susceptible to all kinds of parasites when outside. Make sure he has his proper immunizations before taking him around town.

developing a bloodline. In order to do this, he makes every effort to plan each breeding in regard to conformation, temperament and health. This type of breeder does his best to perform the necessary testing (i.e., OFA, CERF, testing for inherited blood disorders, thyroid, etc.). Testing is expensive and sometimes very disheartening when a favorite dog doesn't pass his health tests. The health history pertains not only to the breeding stock but to the immediate ancestors. Reputable breeders do not want their offspring to be bred indiscriminately. Therefore you may be asked to neuter or spay your puppy. Of course there is

Breeding should only be done by people who have the facilities and knowledge, as well as the means to care for each puppy they produce.

always the exception, and your breeder may agree to let you breed your dog under his direct supervision. This is an important concept. More and more effort is being made to breed healthier dogs.

Spay/Neuter

There are numerous benefits of performing this surgery at six months of age. Unspayed females are subject to mammary and ovarian cancer. In order to prevent mammary cancer she must be spayed prior to her first heat cycle. Later in life, an unspayed

By breeding only the best quality dogs, good temperament and health is passed down to each generation.

female may develop a pyometra (an infected uterus), which is definitely life threatening.

Spaying is performed under a general anesthetic and is easy on the young dog. As you might expect it is a little harder on the older dog, but that is no reason to deny her the surgery. The surgery removes the ovaries and uterus. It is important to remove all the ovarian tissue. If some is left behind, she could remain attractive to males. In order to view the ovaries, a reasonably long incision is necessary. An ovariohysterectomy is considered major surgery.

Neutering the male at a young age will inhibit some characteristic male behavior that owners frown upon. Some boys will not hike their legs and mark territory if they are neutered at six months of age. Also neutering at a young age has hormonal benefits, lessening the chance of hormonal aggressiveness.

Surgery involves removing the testicles but leaving the scrotum. If there should be a retained testicle, then he definitely needs to be neutered before the age of two or three years. Retained testicles can develop into cancer. Unneutered males are at risk for testicular cancer, perineal fistulas, perianal tumors and fistulas and prostatic disease.

Intact males and females are prone to housebreaking accidents. Females urinate frequently before, during and after heat cycles, and males tend to mark territory if there is a female in heat. Males may show the same behavior if there is a visiting dog or guests.

Surgery involves a sterile operating procedure equivalent to human surgery. The incision site is shaved, surgically scrubbed and draped. The veterinarian wears a sterile surgical gown, cap, mask and gloves. Anesthesia should be monitored by a registered technician. It is customary for the veterinarian to recommend a pre-anesthetic blood screening, looking for metabolic problems and a ECG rhythm strip to check for normal heart function. Today anesthetics are equal to human anesthetics, which enables your dog to walk out of the clinic the same day as surgery.

Some folks worry about their dog gaining weight after being neutered or spayed. This is usually not the case. It is true that some dogs may be less active so they could develop a problem, but most dogs are just as active as they were before surgery. However, if your dog should begin to gain, then you need to decrease his food and see to it that he gets a little more exercise.

MEDICAL PROBLEMS

Anal Sacs

These are small sacs on either side of the rectum that can cause the dog discomfort when they are full. They should empty when the dog has a bowel movement. Symptoms of inflammation or impaction are excessive licking under the tail and/or a bloody or sticky discharge from the anal area. Breeders like myself recommend emptying the sacs on a regular schedule when bathing the dog. Many veterinarians prefer this isn't done unless there are symptoms. You can express the sacs by squeezing the two sacs (at the five and seven o'clock positions) in and up toward the anus. Take precautions not to get in the way of the foul-smelling fluid that is expressed. Some dogs object to this procedure so it would be wise to have someone hold the head. Scooting is caused by anal-sac irritation and not worms.

Colitis

The stool may be frank blood or blood tinged and is the result of inflammation of the colon. Colitis, sometimes intermittent, can be the result of stress, undiagnosed whipworms, or perhaps idiopathic (no explainable reason). If intermittent bloody stools are an ongoing problem, you should probably feed a diet higher in fiber. Seek professional help if your dog feels poorly and/or the condition persists.

Conjunctivitis

Many breeds are prone to this problem. The conjunctiva is the pink tissue that lines the inner surface of the eyeball except the clear, transparent cornea. Irritating substances such as bacteria, foreign matter or chemicals can cause it to become reddened and swollen. It is important to keep any hair trimmed from around the eyes. Long hair stays damp and aggravates the problem. Keep the eyes cleaned with warm

Your Shetland Sheepdog's eyes should be clear and free of any redness or irritation.

water and wipe away any matter that has accumulated in the corner of the eyes. If the condition persists, you should see your veterinarian. This problem goes hand in hand with keratoconjunctivitis sicca.

DENTAL CARE for Your Dog's Life

So you've got a new puppy! You also have a new set of puppy teeth in your household. Anyone who has ever raised a puppy is abundantly aware of these new teeth. Your puppy will chew anything it can reach, chase your shoelaces, and play "tear the rag" with any piece of clothing it can find. When puppies are newly born, they have no teeth. At about four weeks of age, puppies of most breeds begin to develop their deciduous or baby teeth. They begin eating semi-solid food, fighting and biting with their litter mates, and learning discipline from their mother. As their new teeth come in, they inflict more pain on their mother's breasts, so her feeding sessions become less frequent and shorter.

Make sure your Sheltie has a safe Nylabone® to play with to satisfy his chewing needs.

By six or eight weeks, the mother will start growling to warn her pups when they are fighting too roughly or hurting her as they nurse too much with their new teeth.

Puppies need to chew. It is a necessary part of their physical and mental development. They develop muscles and necessary life skills as they drag objects around, fight over possession, and vocalize alerts and warnings. Puppies chew on things to explore their world. They are using their sense of taste to determine what is food and what is not. How else can they tell an electrical cord from a lizard? At about four months of age, most puppies begin shedding their baby teeth. Often these teeth need some help to come out and make way for the permanent teeth. The incisors (front teeth) will be replaced

There is only one acceptable material for flossing human teeth and that is nylon. Get a nylon knot like Nylafloss™ upon which your dog can chew and which enables you to interact with your Sheltie by playing tug-of-war.

first. Then, the adult canine or fang teeth erupt. When the baby tooth is not shed before the permanent tooth comes in, veterinarians call it a retained deciduous tooth. This condition will often cause gum infections by trapping hair and debris between the permanent tooth and the retained baby tooth. Nylafloss® is an excellent device for puppies to use. They can toss it, drag it, and chew on the many surfaces it presents. The baby teeth can catch in the nylon material, aiding in their removal. Puppies that have adequate chew toys will have less destructive behavior, develop more physically, and have less chance of retained deciduous teeth.

During the first year, your dog should be seen by your veterinarian at regular intervals. Your veterinarian will let you know when to bring in your puppy for vaccinations and parasite examinations. At each visit,

The Hercules™ is made of very tough polyurethane. It is designed for Shelties that are extra strong chewers. The raised dental tips massage the gums and mechanically remove the plaque during the chewing process.

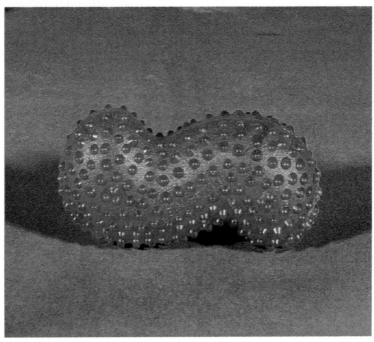

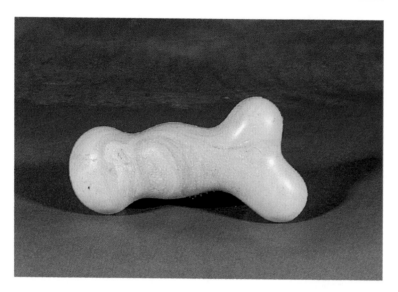

The Galileo™ is the toughest nylon bone ever made. It is flavored to appeal to your Sheltie and annealed so it has a relatively soft outer layer. It is a necessary chew device and Sheltie pacifier.

your veterinarian should inspect the lips, teeth, and mouth as part of a complete physical examination. You should take some part in the maintenance of your dog's oral health. You should examine your dog's mouth weekly throughout his first year to make sure there are no sores, foreign objects, tooth problems, etc. If your dog drools excessively, shakes its head, or has bad breath, consult your veterinarian. By the time your dog is six months old, the permanent teeth are all in and plaque can start to accumulate on the tooth surfaces. This is when your dog needs to develop good dental-care habits to prevent calculus build-up on its teeth. Brushing is best. That is a fact that cannot be denied. However, some dogs do not like their teeth brushed regularly, or you may not be able to accomplish the task. In that case, you should consider a product that will help prevent plaque and calculus build-up.

The Plaque Attackers® and Galileo Bone® are other excellent choices for the first three years of a dog's life. Their shapes make them interesting for the dog. As the dog chews on them, the solid polyurethane massages the gums which improves the blood circulation to the periodontal tissues. Projections on the chew devices increase the surface and are in contact with the tooth for more efficient cleaning. The unique shape and consistency prevent your dog from exerting excessive force on his own teeth or from breaking off pieces of the bone. If your dog is an aggressive chewer or weighs more than 55 pounds (25 kg), you should consider giving him a Nylabone®, the most durable chew product on the market.

The Gumabones ®, made by the Nylabone Company, is constructed of strong polyurethane, which is softer than nylon. Less powerful chewers prefer the Gumabones® to the Nylabones®. A super option for your dog is the Hercules Bone®, a uniquely shaped bone named after the great Olympian for its exception strength. Like all Nylabone products, they are specially scented to make them attractive to your dog. Ask your veterinarian about these bones and he will validate the good doctor's prescription: Nylabones® not only give your dog a good chewing workout but also help to save your dog's teeth (and even his life, as it protects him from possible fatal periodontal diseases).

By the time dogs are four years old, 75% of them have periodontal disease. It is the most common infection in dogs. Yearly examinations by your veterinarian are essential to maintaining your dog's good health. If your veterinarian detects periodontal disease, he or she may recommend a prophylactic cleaning. To do a thorough cleaning, it will be necessary to put your dog under anesthesia. With modern gas anesthetics and monitoring equipment, the procedure is pretty safe. Your veterinarian will scale the teeth with an ultrasound

Raised dental tips help to combat plaque and tartar on the surface of every Plaque Attacker™ bone. Safe for aggressive

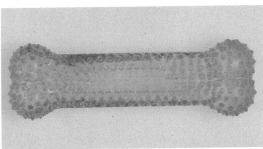

chewers and ruggedly constructed to last, Plaque Attacker™ dental bones provide hours and hours of enjoyment.

scaler or hand instrument. This removes the calculus from the teeth. If there are calculus deposits below the gum line, the veterinarian will plane the roots to make them smooth. After all of the calculus has been removed, the teeth are polished with pumice in a polishing cup. If any medical or surgical treatment is needed, it is done at this time. The final step would be fluoride treatment and your follow-up treatment at home. If the periodontal disease is advanced, the veterinarian may prescribe a medicated

If you take care of your Sheltie's teeth throughout his lifetime, he will always be able to flash a healthy smile.

2-Brush ™ by Nylabone® is made with two toothbrushes to clean both sides of your Sheltie's teeth at the same time. Each brush contains a reservoir designed to apply the toothpaste, which is specially formulated for dogs, directly on to the toothbrush.

mouth rinse or antibiotics for use at home. Make sure your dog has safe, clean and attractive chew toys and treats. Chooz® treats are another way of using a consumable treat to help keep your dog's teeth clean.

Rawhide is the most popular of all materials for a dog to chew. This has never been good news to dog owners, because rawhide is inherently very dangerous for dogs. Thousands of dogs have died from rawhide, having swallowed the hide after it has become soft and mushy, only to cause stomach and intestinal blockage. A new rawhide product on the market has finally solved the problem of rawhide: molded Roar-Hide® from Nylabone. These are composed of processed, cut up, and melted American rawhide injected into your dog's favorite shape: a dog bone. These dog-safe devices smell and taste like rawhide but don't break up. The ridges on the bones help to fight tartar build-up on the teeth and they last ten times longer than the usual rawhide chews.

Chooz™ is a healthy treat for Shelties because they love cheese. This product is bone hard but can be microwaved to make it expand to a crisp dog biscuit. It is practically fat free and contains 70% protein.

As your dog ages, professional examination and cleaning should become more frequent. The mouth should be inspected at least once a year. Your veterinarian may recommend visits every six months. In the geriatric patient, organs such as the heart, liver, and kidneys do not function as well as when they were young. Your veterinarian will probably want to test these organs' functions prior to using general anesthesia for dental cleaning. If

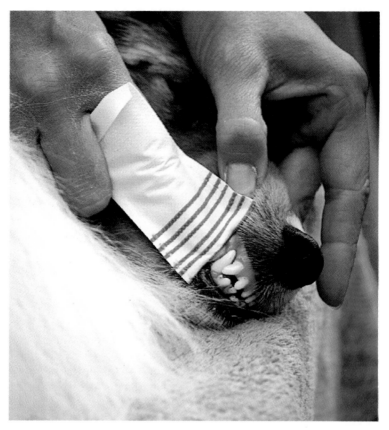

Your grooming regimen should always include cleaning your Sheltie's teeth and examining his mouth.

your dog is a good chewer and you work closely with your veterinarian, your dog can keep all of its teeth all of its life. However, as your dog ages, his sense of smell, sight, and taste will diminish. He may not have the desire to chase, trap or chew his toys. He will also not have the energy to chew for long periods, as arthritis and periodontal disease make chewing painful. This will leave you with more responsibility for keeping his teeth clean and healthy. The dog that would not let you brush his teeth at one year of age, may let you brush his teeth now that he is ten years old.

If you train your dog with good chewing habits as a puppy, he will have healthier teeth throughout his life.

IDENTIFICATION and Finding the Lost Dog

There are several ways of identifying your dog. The old standby is a collar with dog license, rabies, and ID tags. Unfortunately collars have a way of being separated from the dog and tags fall off. We're not suggesting you shouldn't use a collar and tags. If they stay intact and on the dog, they are the quickest way of identification.

For several years owners have been tattooing their dogs. Some tattoos use a number with a registry. Here lies the problem because there are several registries to check. If you wish to tattoo, use your social security number. The humane shelters have the means to trace it. It is usually done on the inside of the rear thigh. The area is first shaved and numbed. There is no pain, although a few dogs do not like the buzzing sound. Occasionally tattooing is not legible and needs to be redone.

The newest method of identification is microchipping. The microchip is a computer chip that is no larger than a grain of rice. The veterinarian implants it by injection between the shoulder blades. The dog feels no discomfort. If your dog is lost and picked up by the humane society, they can trace you by scanning the microchip, which has its own code. Microchip scanners are friendly to other brands of microchips and their registries. The microchip comes with a dog tag saying the dog is microchipped. It is the safest way of identifying your dog.

FINDING THE LOST DOG

I am sure you will agree that there would be little worse than losing your dog. Responsible pet owners rarely lose their dogs. They do not let their dogs run free because they don't want harm to come to them. Not only that but in most, if not all, states there is a leash law.

Beware of fenced-in yards. They can be a hazard. Dogs find ways to escape either over or under the fence. Another fast exit is through the gate that perhaps the neighbor's child left unlocked.

Below is a list that hopefully will be of help to you if you need it. Remember don't give up, keep looking. Your dog is worth your efforts.

1. Contact your neighbors and put flyers with a photo on it in their mailboxes. Information you should include would be the dog's name, breed, sex, color, age, source of identification, when your dog was last seen and where, and your name and phone numbers. It may be helpful to say the dog needs medical care. Offer a *reward*.

Make sure you leave your Shetland Sheepdog in a secured fenced-in area when he is outside and off-lead.

2. Check all local shelters daily. It is also possible for your dog to be picked up away from home and end up in an out-of-the-way shelter. Check these too. Go in person. It is not good enough to call. Most shelters are limited on the time they can hold dogs then they are put up for adoption or euthanized. There is the possibility that your dog will not make it to the shelter for several days. Your dog could have been wandering or someone may have tried to keep him.

3. Notify all local veterinarians. Call and send flyers.

4. Call your breeder. Frequently breeders are contacted when one of their breed is found.

5. Contact the rescue group for your breed.

6. Contact local schools—children may have seen your dog.

7. Post flyers at the schools, groceries, gas stations, convenience stores, veterinary clinics, groomers and any other place that will allow them.

8. Advertise in the newspaper.

9. Advertise on the radio.

TRAVELING with Your Dog

by Judy Iby

The earlier you start traveling with your new puppy or dog, the better. He needs to become accustomed to traveling. However, some dogs are nervous riders and become carsick easily. It is helpful if he starts with an empty stomach. Do not despair, as it will go better if you continue taking him with you on short fun rides. How would you feel if every time you rode in the car you stopped at the doctor's for an injection? You would soon dread that nasty car. Older dogs that tend to get carsick may have more of a problem adjusting to traveling. Those dogs that are having a serious problem may benefit from some medication prescribed by the veterinarian.

Do give your dog a chance to relieve himself before getting into the car. It is a good idea to be prepared for a clean up with a leash, paper towels, bag and terry cloth towel.

The safest place for your dog is in a fiberglass crate, although close confinement can promote carsickness in some dogs. If your dog is nervous you can try letting him ride on the seat next to you or in someone's lap.

An alternative to the crate would be to use a car harness made for dogs and/or a safety strap attached to the harness or collar. Whatever you do, do not let your dog ride in the back of a pickup truck unless he is securely tied on a very short lead.

If you accustom your Sheltie to car rides slowly, he will soon grow to enjoy them.

I've seen trucks stop quickly and, even though the dog was tied, it fell out and was dragged.

Another advantage of the crate is that it is a safe place to leave him if you need to run into the store. Otherwise you wouldn't be able to leave the windows down. Keep in mind that while many dogs are overly protective in their crates, this may not be enough to deter dognappers. In some states it is against the law to leave a dog in the car unattended.

The Sheltie is a very accommodating breed and will happily follow his owner anywhere.

Never leave a dog loose in the car wearing a collar and leash. More than one dog has killed himself by hanging. Do not let him put his head out an open window. Foreign debris can be blown into his eyes. When leaving your dog unattended in a car, consider the temperature. It can take less than five minutes to reach temperatures over 100 degrees Fahrenheit.

TRIPS

Perhaps you are taking a trip. Give consideration to what is best for your dog—traveling with you or boarding. When traveling by car, van or motor home, you need to think ahead about locking your vehicle. In all probability you have many valuables in the car and do not wish to leave it unlocked. Perhaps most valuable and not replaceable is your dog. Give thought to securing your vehicle and providing adequate ventilation for him. Another consideration for you when traveling with your dog is medical problems that may arise and little inconveniences, such as exposure to external parasites. Some areas of the country are quite flea infested. You may want to carry flea spray with you. This is even a good idea when staying in motels. Quite possibly you are not the only occupant of the room.

Unbelievably many motels and even hotels do allow canine guests, even some very first-class ones. Gaines Pet Foods Corporation publishes *Touring With Towser*, a directory of domestic hotels and motels that accommodate guests with dogs. Their address is Gaines TWT, PO Box 5700, Kankakee, IL, 60902. Call ahead to any motel that you may be considering and see if they accept pets. Sometimes it is necessary to pay a deposit against room damage. The management may feel reassured if you mention that your dog will be crated. If you do travel with your dog, take along plenty of baggies so that you can clean up after him. When we all do our share in cleaning up, we make it possible for motels to continue accepting our pets. As a matter of fact, you should practice cleaning up everywhere you take your dog.

Depending on where your are traveling, you may need an up-to-date health certificate issued by your veterinarian. It is good policy to take along your dog's medical information, which would include the name, address and phone number of your veterinarian, vaccination record, rabies certificate, and any medication he is taking.

Air Travel

When traveling by air, you need to contact the airlines to check their policy. Usually you have to make arrangements up to a couple of weeks in advance for traveling with your dog. The airlines require your dog to travel in an airline approved fiberglass crate. Usually these can be purchased through the airlines but they are also readily available in most pet-supply stores. If your dog is not accustomed to a crate, then it is a good idea to get him acclimated to it before your trip. The day of the actual trip you should withhold water about one hour

ahead of departure and no food for about 12 hours. The airlines generally have temperature restrictions, which do not allow pets to travel if it is either too cold or too hot. Frequently these restrictions are based on the

The well-trained and well-socialized Sheltie is a suitable traveling companion for anyone.

You may want to board your dog in a kennel when you go on vacation. However, this Golden Hylite Sheltie pup looks ready for some sun and fun!

temperatures at the departure and arrival airports. It's best to inquire about a health certificate. These usually need to be issued within ten days of departure. You should arrange for non-stop, direct flights and if a commuter plane should be involved, check to see if it will carry dogs. Some don't. The Humane Society of the United States has put together a tip sheet for airline traveling. You can receive a copy by sending a self-addressed stamped envelope to:

The Humane Society of the United States
Tip Sheet
2100 L Street NW
Washington, DC 20037.

Regulations differ for traveling outside of the country and are sometimes changed without notice. Well in advance you need to write or call the appropriate consulate or agricultural department for instructions. Some countries have lengthy quarantines (six months), and countries differ in their rabies vaccination requirements. For instance, it may have to be given at least 30 days ahead of your departure.

Do make sure your dog is wearing proper identification including your name, phone number and city. You never know when you might be in an accident and separated from your dog. Or your dog could be frightened and somehow manage to escape and run away.

Crates are the safest way for your dog to travel in a car.

Another suggestion would be to carry in-case-of-emergency instructions. These would include the address and phone number of a relative or friend, your veterinarian's name, address and phone number, and your dog's medical information.

BOARDING KENNELS

Perhaps you have decided that you need to board your dog. Your veterinarian can recommend a good boarding facility or possibly a pet sitter that will come to your house. It is customary for the boarding kennel to ask for proof of vaccination for the DHLPP, rabies and bordetella vaccine. The bordetella should have been given within six months of boarding. This is for your protection. If they do not ask for this proof I would not board at their kennel. Ask about flea control. Those dogs that suffer flea-bite allergy can get in trouble at a boarding kennel. Unfortunately boarding kennels are limited on how much they are able to do.

For more information on pet sitting, contact NAPPS:
National Association of Professional Pet Sitters
1200 G Street, NW
Suite 760
Washington, DC 20005.

Some pet clinics have technicians that pet sit and technicians that board clinic patients in their homes. This may be an alternative for you. Ask your veterinarian if they have an employee that can help you. There is a definite advantage of having a technician care for your dog, especially if your dog is on medication or is a senior citizen.

When traveling with your Sheltie, be sure to make frequent stops so he can eliminate and get some exercise.

You can write for a copy of *Traveling With Your Pet* from ASPCA, Education Department, 441 E. 92nd Street, New York, NY 10128.

BEHAVIOR and Canine Communication

S tudies of the human/animal bond point out the importance of the unique relationships that exist between people and their pets. Those of us who share our lives with pets understand the special part they play through companionship, service and protection. For many, the pet/owner bond goes beyond simple companionship; pets are often considered members of the family. A leading pet food manufacturer recently conducted a nationwide survey of pet owners to gauge just how important pets were in their lives. Here's what they found:

Spending time with pets has proven to reduce stress and improve the quality of life. Who could help but smile when in the presence of an adorable Sheltie puppy?

- 76 percent allow their pets to sleep on their beds
- 78 percent think of their pets as their children
- 84 percent display photos of their pets, mostly in their homes
- 84 percent think that their pets react to their own emotions
- 100 percent talk to their pets
- 97 percent think that their pets understand what they're saying

Are you surprised?

Senior citizens show more concern for their own eating habits when they have the responsibility of feeding a dog.

Seeing that their dog is routinely exercised encourages the owner to think of schedules that otherwise may seem

The ultimate house dog and companion, the Shetland Sheepdog enriches the lives of his human family.

unimportant to the senior citizen. The older owner may be arthritic and feeling poorly but with responsibility for his dog he has a reason to get up and get moving. It is a big plus if his dog is an attention seeker who will demand such from his owner.

Over the last couple of decades, it has been shown that pets relieve the stress of those who lead busy lives. Owning a pet has been known to lessen the occurrence of heart attack and stroke.

Many single folks thrive on the companionship of a dog. Lifestyles are very different from a long time ago, and today more individuals seek the single life. However, they receive fulfillment from owning a dog.

Most likely the majority of our dogs live in family environments. The companionship they provide is well worth the effort involved. In my opinion, every child should have the opportunity to have a family dog. Dogs

Plenty of play and exercise is not only good for a Sheltie, but can also benefit his owner's health and well being.

teach responsibility through understanding their care, feelings and even respecting their life cycles. Frequently those children who have not been exposed to dogs grow up afraid of dogs, which isn't good. Dogs sense timidity and some will take advantage of the situation.

Today more dogs are serving as service dogs. Since the origination of the Seeing Eye dogs years ago, we now have trained hearing dogs. Also dogs are trained to provide service for the handicapped and are able to perform many different tasks for their owners. Search and Rescue dogs, with their handlers, are sent throughout the world to assist in recovery of disaster victims. They are life savers.

If you introduce your Sheltie to other pets gradually, they will get along famously.

Therapy dogs are very popular with nursing homes, and some hospitals even allow them to visit. The inhabitants truly look forward to their visits. They wanted and were allowed to have visiting dogs in their beds to hold and love.

Nationally there is a Pet Awareness Week to educate students and others about the value and basic care of our pets. Many countries take an even greater interest in their pets than Americans do. In those countries the pets are allowed to accompany their owners into restaurants and shops, etc. In the U.S. this freedom is only available to our service dogs. Even so we think very highly of the human/animal bond.

CANINE BEHAVIOR

Canine behavior problems are the number-one reason for pet owners to dispose of their dogs, either through new homes, humane shelters or euthanasia. Unfortunately there are too many owners who are unwilling to devote the necessary time to properly train their dogs. On the other hand, there are those who not only are concerned about inherited health problems but are also aware of the dog's mental stability.

You may realize that a breed and his group relatives (i.e., sporting, hounds, etc.) show tendencies to behavioral characteristics. An experienced breeder can acquaint you with

Dogs are a very important part of their owners' lives and the bond between humans and animals is a strong one.

his breed's personality. Unfortunately many breeds are labeled with poor temperaments when actually the breed as a whole is not affected but only a small percentage of individuals within the breed.

Inheritance and environment contribute to the dog's behavior. Some naïve people suggest inbreeding as the cause of bad temperaments. Inbreeding only results in poor behavior if the ancestors carry the trait. If there are excellent temperaments behind the dogs, then inbreeding will promote good temperaments in the offspring. Did you ever consider that inbreeding is what sets the characteristics of a breed? A purebred dog is the end result of inbreeding. This does not spare the mixed-breed dog from the same problems. Mixed-breed dogs frequently are the offspring of purebred dogs.

Not too many decades ago most of our dogs led a different lifestyle than what is prevalent today. Usually mom stayed home so the dog had human companionship and someone to discipline it if needed. Not much was expected from the dog. Today's mom works and everyone's life is at a much faster pace.

Watching a Sheltie pup play with his littermates will tell you a lot about his personality. It's easy to see who's top dog around here!

The dog may have to adjust to being a "weekend" dog. The family is gone all day during the week, and the dog is left to his own devices for entertainment. Some dogs sleep all day waiting for their family to come home and others become wigwam wreckers if given the opportunity. Crates do ensure the safety of the dog and the house. However, he could become a physically and emotionally cripple if he doesn't get enough exercise and attention. We still appreciate and want the companionship of our dogs although we expect more from them. In many cases we tend to forget dogs are just that–*dogs* not human beings.

SOCIALIZING AND TRAINING

Many prospective puppy buyers lack experience regarding the proper socialization and training needed to develop the type of pet we all desire. In the first 18 months, training does take some work. It is easier to start proper training before there is a problem that needs to be corrected.

The initial work begins with the breeder. The breeder should start socializing the puppy at five to six weeks of age and cannot let up. Human socializing is critical up through 12 weeks of age and likewise important during the following months. The litter should be left together during the first few weeks but it is necessary to separate them by ten weeks of age. Leaving them together after that time will increase competition for litter dominance. If puppies are not socialized with people by 12 weeks of age, they will be timid in later life.

The eight- to ten-week age period is a fearful time for puppies. They need to be handled very gently around children and adults. There should be no harsh discipline during this time. Starting at 14 weeks of age, the puppy begins the juvenile period, which ends when he reaches sexual maturity around six to 14 months of age.

During the juvenile period he needs to be introduced to strangers (adults, children and other dogs) on the home property. At sexual maturity he will begin to bark at strangers and become more protective. Males start to lift their legs to urinate but if you desire you can inhibit this behavior by walking your boy on leash away from trees, shrubs, fences, etc.

As ancestors of the wolf, the canine instincts will always be evident in the Shetland Sheepdog.

Perhaps you are thinking about an older puppy. You need to inquire about the puppy's social experience. If he has lived in a kennel, he may have a hard time adjusting to people and environmental stimuli. Assuming he has had a good social upbringing, there are advantages to an older puppy.

Training includes puppy kindergarten and a minimum of one to two basic training classes. During these classes you will learn how to dominate your youngster. This is especially important if you own a large breed of dog. It is somewhat harder, if not nearly impossible, for some owners to be the Alpha figure when their dog towers over them. You will be taught how to properly restrain your dog. This concept is important. Again it puts you in the Alpha position. All dogs need to be restrained many times during their lives. Believe it or not, some of our worst offenders are the eight-week-old puppies that are brought to our clinic. They need to be gently restrained for a nail trim but the way they carry on you would think we were killing them. In comparison, their vaccination is a "piece of cake." When we ask dogs to do something that is not agreeable to them, then their worst comes out. Life will be easier for your dog if you expose him at a young age to the necessities of life—proper behavior and restraint.

UNDERSTANDING THE DOG'S LANGUAGE

Most authorities agree that the dog is a descendent of the wolf. The dog and wolf have similar traits. For instance both

are pack oriented and prefer not to be isolated for long periods of time. Another characteristic is that the dog, like the wolf, looks to the leader–Alpha–for direction. Both the wolf and the dog communicate through body language, not only within their pack but with outsiders.

Every pack has an Alpha figure. The dog looks to you, or should look to you, to be that leader. If your dog doesn't receive the proper training and guidance, he very well may replace you as Alpha. This would be a serious problem and is certainly a disservice to your dog.

Eye contact is one way the Alpha wolf keeps order within his pack. You are Alpha so you must establish eye contact with your puppy. Obviously your puppy will have to look at you. Practice eye contact even if you need to hold his head for five to ten seconds at a time. You can give him a treat as a reward. Make sure your eye contact is gentle and not threatening. Later, if he has been naughty, it is permissible to give him a long, penetrating look. There are some older dogs that never learned eye contact as puppies and cannot accept eye contact. You should avoid eye contact with these dogs since they feel threatened and will retaliate as such.

Body Language

The play bow, when the forequarters are down and the hindquarters are elevated, is an invitation to play. Puppies play fight, which helps them learn the acceptable limits of biting. This is necessary for later in their lives. Nevertheless, an owner may be falsely reassured by the playful nature of his dog's aggression. Playful aggression toward another dog or human may be an indication of serious aggression in the future. Owners should never play fight or play tug-of-war with any dog that is inclined to be dominant.

Signs of submission are:

1. Avoids eye contact.
2. Active submission–the dog crouches down, ears back and the tail is lowered.
3. Passive submission–the dog rolls on his side with his hindlegs in the air and frequently urinates.

Signs of dominance are:

1. Makes eye contact.
2. Stands with ears up, tail up and the hair raised on his neck.

3. Shows dominance over another dog by standing at right angles over it.

Dominant dogs tend to behave in characteristic ways such as:

1. The dog may be unwilling to move from his place (i.e., reluctant to give up the sofa if the owner wants to sit there).

2. He may not part with toys or objects in his mouth and may show possessiveness with his food bowl.

Boredom is one of the leading causes of behavior problems such as barking. Make sure your Sheltie is kept occupied with toys when you can't be with him.

3. He may not respond quickly to commands.

4. He may be disagreeable for grooming and dislikes to be petted.

Dogs are popular because of their sociable nature. Those that have contact with humans during the first 12 weeks of life regard them as a member of their own species—their pack. All dogs have the potential for both dominant and submissive behavior. Only through experience and training do they learn to whom it is appropriate to show which behavior. Not all dogs are concerned with dominance but owners need to be aware of that potential. It is wise for the owner to establish his dominance early on.

A human can express dominance or submission toward a dog in the following ways:

1. Meeting the dog's gaze signals dominance. Averting the gaze signals submission. If the dog growls or threatens, averting the gaze is the first avoiding action to take—it may prevent attack. It is important to establish eye contact in the puppy. The older dog that has not been exposed to eye contact may see it as a threat and will not be willing to submit.

2. Being taller than the dog signals dominance; being lower signals submission. This is why, when attempting to make friends with a strange dog or catch the runaway, one should kneel down to his level. Some owners see their

dogs become dominant when allowed on the furniture or on the bed. Then he is at the owner's level.

3. An owner can gain dominance by ignoring all the dog's social initiatives. The owner pays attention to the dog only when he obeys a command.

No dog should be allowed to achieve dominant status over any adult or child. Ways of preventing are as follows:

1. Handle the puppy gently, especially during the three- to four-month period.

2. Let the children and adults handfeed him and teach him to take food without lunging or grabbing.

3. Do not allow him to chase children or joggers.

4. Do not allow him to jump on people or mount their legs. Even females may be inclined to mount. It is not only a male habit.

Dominant dogs may not want to give up their spot for their owners. This Sheltie mom and baby look pretty comfortable on the couch.

Children make great playmates for energetic puppies— and vice versa!

5. Do not allow him to growl for any reason.

6 Don't participate in wrestling or tug-of-war games.

7.   Don't physically punish puppies for aggressive behavior. Restrain him from repeating the infraction and teach an alternative behavior. Dogs should earn everything they receive from their owners. This would include sitting to receive petting or treats, sitting before going out the door and sitting to receive the collar and leash. These types of exercises reinforce the owner's dominance.

Young children should never be left alone with a dog. It is important that children learn some basic obedience commands so they have some control over the dog. They will gain the respect of their dog.

Fear

One of the most common problems dogs experience is being fearful. Some dogs are more afraid than others. On the lesser side, which is sometimes humorous to watch, dogs can be afraid of a strange object. They act silly when something is out of place in the house. We call his problem perceptive intelligence. He realizes the abnormal within his known environment. He does not react the same way in strange environments since he does not know what is normal.

On the more serious side is a fear of people. This can result in backing off, seeking his own space and saying "leave me alone" or it can result in an aggressive behavior that may lead to challenging the person. Respect that the dog wants to be left alone and give him time to come forward. If you approach the cornered dog, he may resort to snapping. If you leave him alone, he may decide to come forward, which should be rewarded with a treat.

A loving and playful relationship with his littermates is the first step to a well-socialized puppy.

Some dogs may initially be too fearful to take treats. In these cases it is helpful to make sure the dog hasn't eaten for about 24 hours. Being a little hungry encourages him to accept the treats, especially if they are of the "gourmet" variety.

Dogs can be afraid of numerous things, including loud noises and thunderstorms. Invariably the owner rewards (by comforting) the dog when it shows signs of fearfulness. When your dog is frightened, direct his attention to something else and act happy. Don't dwell on his fright.

AGGRESSION

Some different types of aggression are: predatory, defensive, dominance, possessive, protective, fear induced, noise provoked, "rage" syndrome (unprovoked aggression), maternal and aggression directed toward other dogs. Aggression is the most common behavioral problem encountered. Protective breeds are expected to be more aggressive than others but with the proper upbringing they can make very dependable companions. You need to be able to read your dog.

Many factors contribute to aggression including genetics and

environment. An improper environment, which may include the living conditions, lack of social life, excessive punishment, being attacked or frightened by an aggressive dog, etc., can all influence a dog's behavior. Even spoiling him and giving too much praise may be detrimental. Isolation and the lack of human contact or exposure to frequent teasing by children or adults also can ruin a good dog.

Lack of direction, fear, or confusion lead to aggression in those dogs that are so inclined. Any obedience exercise, even the sit and down, can direct the dog and overcome fear and/or confusion. Every dog should learn these commands as a youngster, and there should be periodic reinforcement.

When a dog is showing signs of aggression, you should speak calmly (no screaming or hysterics) and firmly give a command that he understands, such as the sit. As soon as your dog obeys, you have assumed your dominant position.

Aggression presents a problem because there may be danger to others. Sometimes it is an emotional issue. Owners may consciously or unconsciously encourage their dog's aggression. Other owners show responsibility by accepting the problem and taking measures to keep it under control. The owner is responsible for his dog's actions, and it is not wise to take a chance on someone being bitten, especially a child. Euthanasia is the solution for some owners and in severe cases this may be the best choice. However, few dogs are that dangerous and very few are that much of a threat to their owners. If caution is exercised and professional help is gained early on, most cases can be controlled.

Some authorities recommend feeding a lower protein (less than 20 percent) diet. They believe this can aid in reducing aggression. If the dog loses weight, then vegetable oil can be added. Veterinarians and behaviorists are having some success with pharmacology. In many cases treatment is possible and can improve the situation.

If you have done everything according to "the book" regarding training and socializing and are still having a behavior problem, don't procrastinate. It is important that the problem gets attention before it is out of hand. It is estimated that 20 percent of a veterinarian's time may be devoted to dealing with problems before they become so intolerable that the dog is separated from its home and owner. If your veterinarian isn't able to help, he should refer you to a behaviorist.

The love, care, and affection you shower on your Shetland Sheepdog will be returned to you over and over again.

SUGGESTED READING

H-1064
Book of the Shetland
Sheepdog
544 pages, black and
white photos.

TW-139
The Proper Care of
Shetland Sheepdogs
2256 pages, over 240
full-color photos.

RE-319
Guide to Owning a
Shetland Sheepdog
64 pages, over 50 full-
color photos.

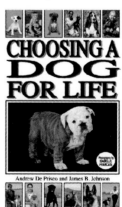

TS-257
Choosing a Dog for Life
384 pages, over 800 full-
color photos.

INDEX